CLEARLY DELICIOUS

CLEARLY DELICIOUS

An Illustrated Guide to Preserving, Pickling, & Bottling

ELISABETH LAMBERT ORTIZ
and
JUDY RIDGWAY

DK Publishing, Inc.

A DORLING KINDERSLEY BOOK

Created and produced by
CARROLL & BROWN LIMITED
5 Lonsdale Road
London NW6 6RA

Editorial Director Jeni Wright
Editors Julia Alcock
Angela Nilsen

Art Editor Chrissie Lloyd
Designers Carmel O'Neill
Michael Dyer

Production Wendy Rogers
Amanda Mackie

First paperback edition, 1998
10 9 8 7 6 5 4 3 2 1

Published in the United States by
DK Publishing, Inc.,
95 Madison Avenue
New York, NY 10016

Ortiz, Elisabeth Lambert
Clearly delicious / by Elisabeth Lambert Ortiz. 1st American
ed.
   p. cm.
Includes index.
ISBN 0-7894-3751-1
1. Canning and preserving. 2. Oils and fats, Edible. 3. Vinegar.
4. Spices. I. Title
TX601.078 1994
641.4--dc20   93-35418
                                                         CIP

Reproduced by Colourscan, Singapore
Printed and bound in Singapore by
Star Standard Industries (Pte.) Ltd.

FOREWORD

THE ART OF PRESERVING can turn an ordinary cupboard or pantry into an Aladdin's cave of good things – beautiful to look at, luscious to eat, and a joy both to give and receive. It can also turn your refrigerator and freezer into a rescue service for emergencies like anniversaries – when homemade presents are obligatory. The kitchen is a cheerful place, and although, undeniably, there is work involved in transforming fruits into jams and jellies, and vegetables into pickles and chutneys, there is no need for lonely drudgery when it comes to preserving. Family, and often friends, like to join in, and what started as a kitchen chore can turn into a celebration with everyone, not just the cook, having fun.

Being creative and economical at the same time can bring a glow of virtue to even the most modest chef. But sometimes imagination flags and the cook is bereft of ideas for a meal that is looming. An array of preserves in the cupboard, refrigerator, or freezer will stimulate culinary wits, and new dishes may well be created by the challenge posed by these good things: new flavors to liven up dull ordinary dishes or simply help familiar ones that need a lift.

The conservation-minded can take special pleasure from reusing jars, bottles, tins, and boxes that would otherwise clutter up kitchen shelves, reproachfully useless. Those artistically gifted with clever fingers can do wonders with gift wrapping, decorating glass jars and bottles, and transforming tins and baskets with ingenuity but little cost. Wrapping paper, labels and tags, ribbons, and cord can all be recruited to help the container be worthy of its contents.

As the Spanish say: *"es mas bueno el vino en bella copa"* – the wine is better in a beautiful glass.

ELISABETH LAMBERT ORTIZ

CONTENTS

INTRODUCTION

The house becomes filled with utterly delectable perfumes when the seasons bring round the time for making preserves.

The practice of "putting up" summer surpluses for winter eating was born of necessity in the days before refrigeration and worldwide imports of fresh fruits and vegetables.

What was then a necessity has today become a pleasure. What can you do with all those tomatoes that ripen at once, or a tree full of fruits, ready for picking before the birds beat you to it, or green beans that will grow in days from delicate little things to tough old monsters?

Transform them by preserving them, enjoy them until the next harvest, and generously give some away. There are so many occasions for parting with a jar from your pantry, refrigerator, or freezer, that it is an excellent idea to put up a lot of good things so as not to run out and find the pantry bare – and with spring an age away. Be as lavish as nature is, a model of generosity. The techniques used in preserving are not difficult, and most kitchens have all the equipment that is needed. Home preserving is a great help to those seeking to avoid additives and preservatives in their food. It is also a great help to the economy-minded, who want luxury foods at a reasonable price, and for the value-conscious, who know they can create specialties at home for a fraction of the cost of the storebought article. The key to successful preserving (in addition to being a creative cook) is always to use the best and freshest ingredients – easy, since both fruits and vegetables are cheapest when they are at their seasonal best, at the most lavish time of harvest.

In these conservation-minded times, we have the added bonus of beautifully designed, modestly priced pressed-glass jars in which to put our preserves and, in addition, equally well-designed jars and bottles that have housed our everyday storebought foods – olives, mustards, capers, spices, and oils, to name but a few. Too pretty and elegantly shaped to throw away, they accumulate on pantry shelves until, washed and with labels removed, they stand ready to be filled with all manner of good things, making us good conservationists as well as good cooks.

But remember, reused bottles and jars without proper seals are suitable for short-term storage only, and are best kept in the refrigerator or freezer. For long-term storage, choose proper preserving containers and lids, and decant your preserves into beautiful bottles to bring to the table or to give as gifts, telling the recipient to store them correctly or eat up quickly!

The occasions for gift-giving are almost endless. There are housewarming gifts, a gift to a new neighbor, gifts to take to a baby shower, a thank-you gift, or one to take to a lunch or dinner party instead of wine, chocolates, or flowers, in fact to any special occasion or festive gathering.

The pleasure of giving and receiving gifts is as old as history, enshrined in legend and tradition, and kept alive principally because it is such a joy. It is a great idea to revive the old-fashioned way of making preserves for gift-giving; transforming fruits and vegetables into pickles, conserves, jams, jellies, curds, marmalades, syrups, flavored vinegars, fruits in alcohol, relishes, chutneys, and more. In addition, the new twist of having modern tools like the food processor and equipment like freezers, lightens your workload. We now have all the world's ingredients to choose from, starting with the herbs in our own gardens, then farms where you can pick your own fruits, to summer and autumn country farm stands, and closer to home our very own greengrocers, specialty food shops, delicatessens, and supermarkets.

Putting up the bounty of summer can take the hassle out of Christmas, especially for those who hate shopping. There is no need for the punishing business of last-minute forays into department stores, or the embarrassment of having forgotten someone when you don't have time to rush out and buy a gift. The holidays are such a wonderful time to part with luxury preserves, like Seville marmalade with almonds, papayas bottled with rum and pistachios, dill pickles with garlic, blueberry-herb vinegar, red currant

jelly with port, or a special liqueur flavored with fruits picked from your own garden.

It is important to label jars and bottles accurately, because it is surprisingly easy to forget which contents are which. The date should always be added, because it is equally easy to forget when they were made. A simple factual label is fine for preserves in the family pantry, refrigerator, or freezer, but for gifts, buy or make labels that will turn the simple jar or bottle into a decorative container. Anyone clever with their hands can use a felt-tip or calligraphy pen to write fancy lettering, while small swatches of patterned fabric tied over the tops of jars with colored ribbon transform even the plainest glass jar into something special. Brightly colored jams, jellies, and preserved whole fruits are often attractive enough in themselves that they need no further embellishment. However, decorating your containers is fun, and a rewarding finishing touch to the fruits of your labor.

BEAUTIFUL BOTTLES

The rich colors and enticing appearance of preserves are best exploited by displaying them in glass containers. Glass is an excellent material, because it does not react with any of the ingredients used, and tolerates careful heating. All kinds of attractive and unusual shapes are available, and any type of reasonably thick glass bottle or jar can be used, in addition to specialized preserving jars, which are more suitable for long-term storage. Whatever containers you choose, they must be scrupulously clean before use. The size and shape of bottles and jars are often dictated by the type of preserves you are making. Large jars with wide necks are needed for packing whole fruits, whereas 12 oz jars are more useful for jams, marmalades, and chutneys.

Sterilizing Containers

Before you start making any preserve, it is important that all bottles, jars, and lids be clean, free of cracks, and sterile. The following is a step-by-step guide to the sterilizing technique.

☙ Clean off all labels (if reusing containers) and wash the bottles, jars, and lids in hot water with detergent. Rinse thoroughly in hot water.

☙ Put a wire rack in the bottom of a large deep saucepan, and place the bottles and jars on it.

☙ Pour in enough water to cover the bottles and jars. Bring to a boil and boil rapidly for 10 minutes. Remove from the water with sterilized tongs and turn them upside down on a thick kitchen towel to drain. Scald the lids.

☙ Preheat the oven to 225°F. Dry the sterilized bottles and jars in the oven. They can be kept warm in the oven until needed or, if the recipe requires putting the preserve into a cold container, leave them to cool. Leave the lids to dry thoroughly on a kitchen towel.

Sterilizing filled containers

The boiling water bath is the most reliable method of sealing, by using glass canning jars fitted with two-piece screw-top lids. These create an airtight seal when processed in the hot water bath, destroy micro-organisms, and give the contents of the jars a good shelf life in different climatic conditions.

☙ Fill the sterilized jars with the chosen preserve, to within 1/8 inch of the tops. Wipe the rim of the jar. Put on the sterilized disk lids, and screw the top on tightly.

☙ Place a wire rack in the base of a larger deep saucepan. Stand the filled jars right-side up on the rack, making sure there is plenty of room between each one and that they do not touch the sides of the pan. Pour water into the pan to cover the jars by 1/4 inch. Cover the pan and bring to simmering point (190°F). Keep the water at this temperature, for the following timings: jams, jellies, marmalades, butters, and spreads, 5–10 minutes; preserves and conserves, 20–30 minutes; pickles, 10–15 minutes; relishes, 15–20 minutes.

☙ Carefully lift the jars out with tongs. Leave to cool completely. You will hear a soft "plink" which means a strong vacuum has formed and the jars are sealed.

Stand the bottles and jars right-side up on a wire rack in the saucepan, making sure they do not touch either the sides of the pan or each other.

All lids should be scalded in a saucepan of boiling water before using. Lower the lids into the boiling water with a pair of tongs to eliminate the risk of burning hands.

Dry the sterilized jars right-side up on a baking sheet, in a preheated oven. This will take about 15 minutes. Do not increase the heat, because the glass may crack under pressure.

JAMS,
JELLIES
& OTHER SWEET
CONCOCTIONS

JAMS

SUMMER HERALDS the joyous beginning of jam making, when the house is filled with the perfume of simmering fruits being transformed by sugar and heat into a luscious spread. Jam turns bread into a luxury and is a useful ingredient in sauces, and desserts, such as cakes and cookies. There is hardly a sight more enticing than an abundance of fruits waiting to be transformed into jam. With a great cornucopia of fruits to choose from, swelling and ripening in a tantalizing succession of harvest, throughout summer and autumn, there is plenty of room for experimentation.

Although familiar fruits, such as raspberries and strawberries, still provide the most popular jams, less traditional flavors can be created with pineapples, or apples and ginger. Indeed, part of the fun, when filling jars with the finished jam, is to admire the colors produced by the clever blending of fruits. Rhubarb and strawberries, for instance, combine to make a beautiful rose-red confection, pleasing both eye and palate.

MAKING JAMS

❧ Choose the ingredients. Jam is made with two main ingredients – fruit and sugar. The fruit must contain the right proportions of pectin and acid so that the jam can set properly, and enough sugar must be added to preserve it. (Pectin is a natural strengthening substance found only in fruits.) Fruits that are fresh and slightly underripe contain the most pectin, so buy or pick the desired fruits when they are just coming into season. Overripe fruits contain very little pectin, so they do not set well, and are better kept for making chutneys. Fruits high in both pectin and acid are cooking apples, cranberries, gooseberries, currants, and some plums. Fruits that will set a jam moderately well are blackberries, greengage plums, apricots, loganberries, and raspberries. Cherries, pears, pineapples, nectarines, and some varieties of strawberry are poor setters and need the addition of pectin and acid to make a satisfactory jam. Fruits that do not have good setting properties can be used in combination with those that do, such as pears with damsons, and raspberries with the addition of red currants; these combinations may also require an acid such as lemon juice. Alternatively, commercial liquid or powdered fruit pectin can be useful for adding to jams made with ingredients low in pectin. It is important to add the correct amount, so follow the manufacturer's instructions carefully. Dried fruits like apricots make very good jam, provided they have not been preserved with sulfur dioxide, which can affect the set. They need to be soaked for at least 24 hours before cooking. Some vegetables, such as carrots, can be used to make jam, but they need plenty of added lemon juice to ensure a reasonable set and may require extra flavorings, such as spices.

❧ When it comes to the choice of sugar, both refined cane and beet granulated sugars work well, and there is no difference in the keeping qualities of jam made from either of these. However, lump sugar is better because it forms less scum and also gives a slightly brighter, clearer jam. Raw (turbinado) or brown sugar can be used when a darker, stronger color and flavor are required.

❧ Other ingredients, such as nuts and a few tablespoons of liqueur or spirit, can be added to make the jams more interesting. These should be stirred in at the last minute after skimming the jam.

❧ Prepare the fruits. Remove any stalks, leaves, moldy or bruised parts. Wash lightly and pat dry with paper towels, to remove excess water. Pitted fruits should be halved and their pits removed. Some recipes call for the addition of a few kernels which are found inside the pits of fruits. Extract the kernels by cracking the pits with a hammer. Adding a few kernels will give the jam extra flavor, but too

many will make the jam bitter. Blanch the kernels in boiling water and remove their skins before adding to the fruits.

❧ Measure out the ingredients carefully, because successful jam setting depends on maintaining the proper proportions of ingredients.

❧ Put the prepared fruits into a preserving pan with the recommended amount of water, and simmer until the fruits are soft. Generally, to ensure a good set the mixture should reduce by about one-third before the sugar is added. Start the juices running in soft fruits by crushing some of the fruits in the bottom of the pan with a potato masher.

❧ Warm the sugar (see box, page 20) while the fruits are cooking. Although this is not essential, the sugar will dissolve more quickly when warm rather than when cold. Make sure the fruits are thoroughly softened; if the sugar is added too soon, it will have a hardening effect on the fruits and this cannot be rectified. Add all of the sugar at once and stir over low heat until it has completely dissolved. A pat of butter can be added at this point to help reduce foaming. Increase the heat and bring to a boil as quickly as possible, then simmer until setting point is reached. Stir the jam as little as possible after the sugar has dissolved.

❧ Test the jam for setting, removing it from the heat first to prevent overcooking. The best way to test is with a candy thermometer. If you can, clip it to the side of the pan when you start to cook the fruits. You will then be able to read the temperature as the jam cooks. If this is not possible, heat the thermometer in a container of hot water. Stir the jam and immerse the bulb of the thermometer completely in the jam, taking care not to let it touch the bottom of the pan. When the thermometer reads 220°F, the jam should set if you have followed the recipe carefully.

❧ You can also test the jam by dropping a little onto a cold plate. This is known as the cold plate or saucer test. Chill quickly in the refrigerator.

If the jam forms a skin, and wrinkles when it is pushed with a finger or spoon, it has reached setting point.

❧ When setting point is reached, lightly skim off any froth with a long-handled metal spoon. Pour the jam into dry sterilized jars (see page 11). Fill the jars, to within ¹/₈ inch of the tops. If directed in the recipe, leave whole fruit jams to stand to cool slightly, before putting into jars, so that a thin skin forms and the fruits are evenly distributed through the jam.

How to seal and store
Seal the jars tightly either with screw-top lids or with lids made of separate screwbands. You can also seal the jars with melted paraffin. Heat the paraffin in the top of a double boiler or in a pan over very low heat until just melted. Transfer it to a heatproof measuring cup with a spout and pour it onto the cooled jam to make a layer less than ¹/₄ inch thick. (Add the paraffin while the jam is still hot if commercial pectin has been used.) Leave the wax to cool, then use a sterilized needle to prick any air pockets in the soft, hot wax. When the wax has cooled, cover the jars with a protective lid or a paper cover to keep the dust and spoilers away. Label the jars and keep in a cool dark place or in the refrigerator.

What can go wrong and why
A jam will crystallize if an over concentration of sugar has been caused by excessive boiling. Jam can ferment or go moldy if it contains too little sugar, or if it was not boiled sufficiently. This also happens as a result of poor storage conditions, or through using overripe, wet or bad fruits, or wet jars. If the jam is very dark, it has probably been boiled too quickly at the first stage or too slow at the sugar stage. Storage in too bright a light also darkens jam. If the setting point has not been reached, the jam will be runny. It can be corrected by returning the runny jam to the preserving pan and reboiling. Alternatively, add commercial pectin and follow the package instructions carefully. Too much pectin will spoil the flavor. Other setting problems can be caused by a lack of pectin or acid in the jam, or by underboiling the fruits so that the pectin is not fully released.

EQUIPMENT

*Jam making requires little in the way of specialized equipment.
The most worthwhile investment for the avid jam maker is a
good-quality preserving pan. Most of the other items shown here
are pieces of everyday equipment.*

**CITRUS FRUIT
SQUEEZER**

WEIGHING SCALES

MEASURING CUP
*Plastic, glass, ceramic,
or stainless steel
measuring cups are all
suitable. Other metals
should be avoided,
particularly if vinegar
is being used.*

LADLE

CANDY THERMOMETER

**STAINLESS
STEEL
SPOON**
*Plain or slotted
for skimming.*

**CUTTING BOARD, SHARP
STAINLESS STEEL KNIVES,
AND VEGETABLE PEELER**

**MEASURING
SPOONS**

MUSLIN
For wrapping up spices or pith and pips, and for straining.

WOODEN SPOONS
Choose long-handled ones so that the hot preserve doesn't splash your hand.

DID YOU KNOW?
A wide variety of jam jars and closures are readily available. The most effective container for long-term storage is a glass jar with a screw-top lid, because the lid is airtight. Wax and cellophane circles are also very useful for covering jams on a short-term basis. The circle of wax is placed on the jam, wax-side down, and smoothed over carefully with a fingertip to remove any air pockets that may be trapped between the jam and the wax circle. A damp cellophane circle is then placed over the jar and firmly secured with a rubber band.

PLASTIC SIEVES
Metal sieves can give an unpleasant flavour to jam, so always use plastic ones.

LABELS

PRESERVING PAN
A wide, fairly shallow preserving pan, made of good-quality stainless steel, is best for rapid boiling of fruit and sugar. Avoid brass or copper, unless specified in the recipe.

CONTAINERS
Use sterilized and dried jars and closures.

FUNNELS
Essential for pouring liquids from one container to another, especially bottles with narrow necks.

PLUM AND WALNUT JAM

Late summer is the time to make this jam, and plums, in all their different hues, offer a wide choice of colors. Try blending red and yellow plums to give a deep shade of pink to your jars of jam. Chopped nuts stirred in at the last minute make an interesting addition.

INGREDIENTS

2 lb red plums

2 lb yellow plums

1 3/4 cups water

9 cups sugar,
warmed (see box, page 20)

2 cups walnuts, roughly
chopped

Makes about 2 quarts

1 ◄ Halve and pit the plums. Crack a few of the pits with a hammer and take out the kernels. Discard the rest.

2 Put the kernels into a bowl and pour over boiling water to cover. Leave for 1 minute, then drain and transfer to a bowl of cold water. Drain again, and rub off the skins.

3 ◄ Put the plums, kernels, and measured water into a preserving pan and bring to a boil. Lower the heat and simmer, stirring occasionally, for 30–40 minutes or until the plum skins are soft and the fruit is tender. The mixture in the pan should have reduced by about one-third.

4 ◄ Add the warmed sugar, and stir over low heat, until the sugar has completely dissolved. Boil the mixture rapidly, without stirring, for 10 minutes or until it reaches setting point. Remove the pan from the heat to test.

5 ▼ The candy thermometer should read 220°F. If you do not have a thermometer, test for setting with the cold plate test (see page 15). Lightly skim off any froth, using a long-handled metal spoon.

6 ▲ Stir in the walnuts. Immediately pour the jam into warmed sterilized jars, to within ⅛ inch of the tops. Seal the jars and label.

LATTICED PLUM PIE
Plum and Walnut Jam fills this luscious tart, topped with a decorative lattice of pastry.

PEACH JAM

INGREDIENTS

3 lb peaches

1 cup water

7¹/₂ cups sugar

¹/₄ cup lemon juice

one 3 oz package liquid
fruit pectin

Most liquid fruit pectin is made from the white pulp under the skin of citrus fruits, but it can also be made from apples.

1 Halve, pit, peel, and dice the peaches. You should have 4 cups of diced peaches. Crack a few of the pits with a hammer and take out the kernels. Discard the rest. Put the kernels in a bowl and pour boiling water over them to cover. Leave for 1 minute, then drain and transfer to a bowl of cold water. Drain again, and rub off the skins with your fingers.

2 Put the peaches, kernels, and the water into a preserving pan and bring to a boil. Lower the heat and simmer, stirring occasionally, for 20–30 minutes or until the peaches are soft. Add the sugar, lemon juice, and pectin, and stir, with a wooden spoon, until the sugar has completely dissolved.

3 Increase the heat and boil the mixture rapidly, without stirring, for only 1 minute or according to package instructions. With the pan off the heat, lightly skim off any froth from the surface of the jam, using a long-handled metal spoon. Cool slightly.

4 Pour the jam into warmed sterilized jars, to within ¹/₈ inch of the tops. Seal the jars and label.

Makes about 2 quarts

DID YOU KNOW?
Jam will not set without pectin, which is a setting agent found naturally, in varying degrees, in most fruits. Jam recipes made with fruits that are low in pectin are best made with a commercially bought liquid pectin to ensure a good set.

PEAR AND DAMSON PLUM JAM

INGREDIENTS

2 lb pears

2 lb damson plums

1¹/₄ cups water

9 cups sugar, warmed
(see box, below)

1 Halve, core, peel, and dice the pears. Put the peel and cores on a square of cheesecloth and tie up tightly into a bag with a long piece of string. Put the diced pears, damson plums, and water into a preserving pan, tie the cheesecloth bag to the pan handle, and bring to a boil.

2 Lower the heat, and simmer, stirring occasionally, for 1 hour or until the plum skins are soft and the fruit is tender. The mixture in the pan should have reduced by about one-third. Skim off and discard the damson pits with a slotted spoon as they come to the surface. Discard the bag, squeezing it first to extract all the juice.

3 Add the warmed sugar to the fruit mixture, and stir over low heat, until the sugar has completely dissolved.

4 Increase the heat and boil the mixture rapidly, without stirring, for 10 minutes or until it reaches setting point. Continue to skim off the pits from the top. Remove the pan from the heat to test. The candy thermometer should read 220°F. Alternatively, test for setting with the cold plate test (see page 15).

5 With the pan off the heat, lightly skim off any remaining pits and any froth from the surface of the jam, using a long-handled metal spoon.

6 Pour the jam into warmed sterilized jars, to within ¹/₈ inch of the tops. Seal the jars and label.

Makes about 7 cups

WARMING SUGAR Sugar will dissolve quickly in the fruit mixture if it is warmed first. Put the oven on its lowest setting. Weigh the sugar and put it into an ovenproof bowl. Warm the sugar in the oven for about 15 minutes. The sterilized jars can be put into the oven to warm at the same time.

CRUSHED STRAWBERRY JAM

INGREDIENTS

4 quarts strawberries

6 Tb lemon juice

*7¹/₂ cups sugar, warmed
(see box, page 20)*

WHOLE STRAWBERRY JAM Leave whole hulled strawberries to stand with the lemon juice and cold sugar overnight. Put the mixture into a preserving pan, heat gently, and continue as directed from step 4. Leave 15 minutes before putting into jars.

1 Hull the strawberries and check their weight. You should have 4 lb of hulled fruit. Halve the strawberries and put them in a nonmetallic bowl. Lightly crush them with a potato masher.

2 Put the crushed strawberries and lemon juice into a preserving pan and bring to a boil. Lower the heat and simmer for 5–10 minutes or until the strawberries are soft.

3 Add the warmed sugar to the strawberry mixture, and stir over low heat, until the sugar has completely dissolved.

4 Increase the heat and boil the mixture rapidly, without stirring, for 15 minutes or until it reaches setting point. Remove the pan from the heat to test. The candy thermometer should read 220°F. If you do not have a candy thermometer, test for setting with the cold plate test (see page 15).

5 With the pan off the heat, lightly skim off any froth from the surface of the jam, using a long-handled metal spoon. Cool the jam slightly.

6 Pour the jam into warmed sterilized jars, to within ¹/₈ inch of the tops. Seal the jars and label.

Makes about 7 cups

BRANDIED CARROT JAM

INGREDIENTS

2 lb young carrots

3²/₃ cups water

*3¹/₃ cups sugar, warmed
(see box, page 20)*

*finely grated zest and juice of
2 large lemons*

1 Tb freshly grated gingerroot

2 Tb brandy

1 Trim, peel, and coarsely chop the carrots. Put the carrots and water into a preserving pan and bring to a boil. Lower the heat and simmer, covered, for 20 minutes or until the carrots are very soft. Purée the carrots in a food processor or blender. Alternatively, press them through a plastic sieve.

2 Return the carrots to the pan. Add the warmed sugar, lemon zest and juice, and grated ginger to the carrot mixture. Stir over low heat until the sugar has completely dissolved.

3 Increase the heat and boil the mixture rapidly, without stirring, for 15–20 minutes or until it reaches setting point. Remove the pan from the heat to test. The candy thermometer should read 220°F. If you do not have a candy thermometer, test for setting with the cold plate test (see page 15).

4 With the pan off the heat, lightly skim off any froth from the surface of the jam, using a long-handled metal spoon. Stir in the brandy.

5 Immediately pour the jam into warmed sterilized jars, to within ¹/₈ inch of the tops. Seal the jars and label.

Makes about 2 cups

BLUEBERRY JAM

INGREDIENTS

4 lb blueberries

7 cups sugar

juice of 2 lemons

pinch of salt

Sweet spicy blueberries are high in pectin so they are the perfect fruit for jam making. Fresh blueberries are available during the summer and early autumn months.

1 Put the blueberries into a nonmetallic bowl with half of the sugar, all of the lemon juice, and the salt. Stir to mix, cover, and leave to stand for about 5 hours or overnight.

2 Pour the contents of the bowl into a preserving pan. Add the remaining sugar, and stir over low heat, with a wooden spoon, until the sugar has completely dissolved.

3 Increase the heat and boil the mixture rapidly, without stirring, for 10–12 minutes or until it reaches setting point. Remove the pan from the heat to test. The candy thermometer should read 220°F. If you do not have a candy thermometer, test for setting with the cold plate test (see page 15).

4 With the pan off the heat, lightly skim off any froth from the surface of the jam, using a long-handled metal spoon.

5 Immediately pour the jam into warmed sterilized jars, to within ⅛ inch of the tops. Seal the jars and label.

Makes about 9 cups

RASPBERRY AND RED CURRANT JAM

INGREDIENTS

1 cup red currants

4 cups water

4 lb raspberries

11 cups sugar, warmed
(see box, page 20)

1 Put the red currants into a preserving pan over low heat. When the juices start to run, add the water. Increase the heat and bring to a boil, then lower the heat and simmer, stirring occasionally, for 15 minutes.

2 Strain the red currants through a plastic sieve into a large measuring cup, pressing with the back of a wooden spoon to extract all the juice. Discard the pulp in the sieve. The juice should measure 3 cups, so reduce it if necessary by boiling it longer.

3 Pour the red currant juice back into the pan. Add the raspberries and bring to a boil. Lower the heat and simmer for 10 minutes. Add the warmed sugar to the mixture, and stir until the sugar has completely dissolved.

4 Increase the heat and boil the mixture rapidly, without stirring, for 10–15 minutes or until it reaches setting point. Remove the pan from the heat to test. The candy thermometer should read 220°F. Alternatively, test for setting with the cold plate test (see page 15).

5 With the pan off the heat lightly skim off any froth from the surface of the jam, using a long-handled metal spoon. Immediately pour the jam into warmed sterilized jars, to within ⅛ inch of the tops. Seal the jars and label.

Makes about 9 cups

*From left to right,
Blueberry Jam,
Pineapple Jam, and
Raspberry and
Red Currant Jam*

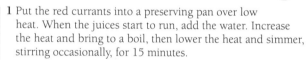

Blackberry and Apple Jam

INGREDIENTS

2 lb cooking apples

1¹/₁ cups water

4 lb blackberries

14 cups sugar, warmed
(see box, page 20)

1 Peel, core, and roughly chop the apples. You should have about 1¹/₂ lb in weight. Put the apples and half of the water into a medium saucepan. Bring to a boil, lower the heat, and simmer, stirring occasionally, for about 10 minutes or until the apples are very soft. Set aside.

2 Put the blackberries and the remaining water into a preserving pan. Bring to a boil, and simmer for about 15 minutes or until the blackberries are soft. Add the apples and return to a boil. Add the warmed sugar to the fruit mixture, and stir with a wooden spoon until the sugar has completely dissolved.

3 Increase the heat and boil the mixture rapidly, without stirring, for about 10 minutes, or until it reaches setting point. Remove the pan from the heat to test. The candy thermometer should read 220°F. If you do not have a candy thermometer, test for setting with the cold plate test (see page 15).

4 With the pan off the heat, lightly skim off any froth from the surface of the jam, using a long-handled metal spoon. Immediately pour the jam into warmed sterilized jars, to within ¹/₈ inch of the tops. Seal the jars and label.

Makes about 13 cups

Pineapple Jam

INGREDIENTS

2 ripe pineapples, total weight
about 3 lb with leaves

5 cups sugar

about 2 lemons

1 Slice the tops off the pineapples. Cut off the peel in strips, cutting deep enough to remove the "eyes" with the peel. Cut the pineapples across into thick slices and cut out and discard the hard center core from each slice; dice the flesh. Weigh the fruit. For each 1 lb fruit, measure 2 cups sugar. Put the fruit into a saucepan. Warm the sugar (see box, page 20), and add it to the pan.

2 Allow 1 lemon for each 1 lb fruit. Peel off the zest and slice it finely. Halve and squeeze the lemons, keeping the seeds and juice for later use. Roughly chop the squeezed lemon halves. Put them with the seeds on a square of cheesecloth and tie up tightly into a bag with a long piece of string.

3 Put the lemon zest and juice in the pan with the pineapple and tie the cheesecloth bag to the pan handle. Stir the mixture over a low heat, until the sugar has completely dissolved. Increase the heat and bring to a boil, then simmer, stirring occasionally, for about 1¹/₂ hours. Remove the pan from the heat. Test for setting with the cold plate test (see page 15). It will be a lighter set than most jams. Discard the cheesecloth bag, squeezing it first to extract all the juice.

4 With the pan off the heat, lightly skim off any froth from the surface of the jam, using a long-handled metal spoon. Immediately pour the jam into warmed sterilized jars, to within ¹/₈ inch of the tops. Seal the jars and label.

Makes about 1 quart

Nectarine Jam

INGREDIENTS

3 lb nectarines

²/₃ cup water

7¹/₂ cups sugar

¹/₄ cup lemon juice

one 3 oz package liquid
fruit pectin

Nectarines, like peaches, are low in pectin, so it is easier to achieve a set with this jam if commercial liquid fruit pectin is added. When using this pectin, lemon juice must be added and the jam must not cook for too long because it reaches setting point quickly and overcooking reduces the pectin's setting properties.

1 Halve and pit the nectarines, but do not peel them. Chop them coarsely.

2 Put the chopped nectarines and water into a preserving pan, and simmer for 15 minutes or until the fruit is soft.

3 Crush the chopped nectarines with a potato masher. Add the sugar, lemon juice, and pectin to the nectarine mixture, and stir over low heat until the sugar has completely dissolved.

4 Increase the heat and boil the mixture rapidly, without stirring, for only 1 minute or according to package instructions.

5 With the pan off the heat, lightly skim off any froth from the surface of the jam, using a long-handled metal spoon. Cool the jam slightly.

6 Immediately pour the jam into warmed sterilized jars, to within ¹/₈ inch of the tops. Seal the jars and label.

COOK'S TIP Use a small sharp knife to remove pits from fruits. Using the indentation on one side as a guide, cut the fruit in half. Then with both hands, give a sharp twist to each half to loosen the pit. Lift or scoop out the pit with the knife.

Makes about 2 cups

Loganberry Jam

INGREDIENTS

6 lb loganberries

juice of 1 lemon

14 cups sugar, warmed
(see box, page 20)

1 Put the loganberries and lemon juice into a preserving pan. Simmer over a medium heat, stirring, until the juices run free. Bring the mixture to a boil, then lower the heat and simmer, stirring occasionally, for 15–20 minutes or until the fruit is soft.

2 Add the warmed sugar to the loganberry mixture, and stir with a wooden spoon until the sugar has completely dissolved.

3 Increase the heat and boil the mixture rapidly, without stirring, for 4–6 minutes or until it reaches setting point. Remove the pan from the heat to test. The candy thermometer should read 220°F. If you do not have a candy thermometer, test for setting with the cold plate test (see page 15).

4 With the pan off the heat, lightly skim off any froth from the surface of the jam, using a long-handled metal spoon.

5 Immediately pour the jam into warmed sterilized jars, to within ¹/₈ inch of the tops. Seal the jars and label.

VARIATIONS
Raspberries can be used in place of loganberries. Alternatively, try using dewberries, boysenberries, blackberries, or even a mixture of berries. Wild or freshly picked ones give jams the best flavor.

Makes about 3 quarts

RHUBARB AND STRAWBERRY JAM

INGREDIENTS

3 lb rhubarb

about 1 quart (1 lb) strawberries

7 cups sugar

3 lemons

Above, Rhubarb and Strawberry Jam; **right,** Fresh Apricot Jam

Rhubarb and strawberries combined together make a wonderfully scented chunky jam.

1 Trim the rhubarb and cut the stalks into ¹/₈ inch pieces. Hull and halve the strawberries. Layer the fruit pieces with the sugar in a large nonmetallic bowl. Halve and squeeze the lemons, keeping the seeds, juice, and lemon halves. Pour the juice over the layered fruit. Cover and leave to stand overnight to draw out the juices.

2 Roughly chop the squeezed lemon halves. Place the fruit with the seeds on a square of cheesecloth. Tie up tightly into a bag with a long piece of string. Pour the contents of the bowl into a preserving pan. Tie the cheesecloth bag to the pan handle, so that it rests on the fruit.

3 Bring the mixture to a boil over a high heat and boil rapidly, without stirring, for 15 minutes or until it reaches setting point. Remove the pan from the heat to test. The candy thermometer should read 220°F. If you do not have a candy thermometer, test for setting with the cold plate test (see page 15). Lift the bag out of the pan and squeeze all the juice back into the pan. Discard the bag.

4 With the pan off the heat, lightly skim off any froth from the surface of the jam, using a long-handled metal spoon. Immediately pour the jam into warmed sterilized jars, to within ¹/₈ inch of the tops. Seal the jars and label.

Makes about 6 cups

FRESH APRICOT JAM

INGREDIENTS

6 lb apricots

2¹/₃ cups water

juice of 1 lemon

14 cups sugar, warmed (see box, page 20)

1 Halve and pit the apricots. Crack a few of the pits with a hammer and take out the kernels. Discard the rest. Put the kernels into a small bowl and pour boiling water over them to cover. Leave for 1 minute, then drain and transfer to a bowl of cold water. Drain again, then rub off the skins with your fingers.

2 Put the apricots, kernels, measured water, and lemon juice into a preserving pan and bring to a boil. Lower the heat and simmer, stirring occasionally, for 20–30 minutes or until the apricot skins are soft and the fruit is tender. The mixture in the pan should have reduced by about one-third. Add the warmed sugar to the mixture and stir until the sugar has completely dissolved.

3 Increase the heat and boil, without stirring, for 10 minutes or until it reaches setting point. Remove the pan from the heat to test. The candy thermometer should read 220°F. Alternatively, test for setting with the cold plate test (see page 15).

4 With the pan off the heat, lightly skim off any froth from the surface of the jam, using a long-handled metal spoon. Immediately pour the jam into warmed sterilized jars, to within ¹/₈ inch of the tops. Seal the jars and label.

Makes about 3 quarts

BLACKCURRANT JAM

INGREDIENTS

8 cups blackcurrants

5^1/$_2$ cups water

14 cups sugar, warmed
(see box, page 20)

Blackcurrants are the ideal fruit for jam making as they have a high level of pectin. Remove them from their stalks with a fork.

1 Put the blackcurrants and water into a preserving pan and bring to a boil. Lower the heat and simmer, stirring occasionally with a wooden spoon, for 50–60 minutes, or until the blackcurrant skins are soft and the fruit is tender. The fruit mixture should have reduced by about one-third.

2 Add the warmed sugar to the blackcurrant mixture, and stir over low heat, until the sugar has completely dissolved.

3 Increase the heat and boil the mixture rapidly, without stirring, for 6–8 minutes or until it reaches setting point. (This jam reaches setting point quickly, so start testing early.) Remove the pan from the heat to test. The candy thermometer should read 220°F. If you do not have a candy thermometer, test for setting with the cold plate test (see page 15).

4 With the pan off the heat, lightly skim off any froth from the surface of the jam, using a long-handled metal spoon.

5 Immediately pour the jam into warmed sterilized jars, to within ^{1}/$_8$ inch of the tops. Seal the jars and label.

Makes about 9 cups

GREENGAGE PLUM JAM

INGREDIENTS

4^1/$_2$ lb greengage plums

1^3/$_4$ cups water

9 cups sugar, warmed
(see box, page 20)

1 Halve and pit the plums and check their weight. You should have 4 lb pitted fruit. Crack a few of the pits with a hammer and take out the kernels. Discard the rest. Put the kernels into a small bowl and pour boiling water over them to cover. Leave for 1 minute, then drain and transfer to a small bowl of cold water. Drain again, then rub off the skins with your fingers.

2 Put the plums, kernels, and measured water into a copper or brass pan and bring to a boil. Lower the heat and simmer, stirring occasionally, for 30–40 minutes or until the plum skins are soft and the fruit is tender. The mixture in the pan should have reduced by about one-third.

3 Add the warmed sugar to the plum mixture, and stir over low heat, with a wooden spoon, until the sugar has completely dissolved.

4 Increase the heat and boil the mixture rapidly, without stirring, for 10 minutes or until it reaches setting point. Remove the pan from the heat to test. The candy thermometer should read 220°F. If you do not have a candy thermometer, test for setting with the cold plate test (see page 15).

5 With the pan off the heat, lightly skim off any froth from the surface of the jam, using a long-handled metal spoon.

6 Pour the jam into warmed sterilized jars, to within ^{1}/$_8$ inch of the tops. Seal the jars and label.

Makes about 7 cups

DID YOU KNOW? Jams made with greengage plums and gooseberries tend to discolor when made in a stainless steel pan. Use a copper or brass pan instead.

Apple and Ginger Jam

Ingredients

6 lb cooking apples

4¹/₂ cups water

2 tsp ground ginger

finely grated zest and juice of
1 lemons

¹/₂ cup candied ginger or
ginger in syrup

12 cups sugar, warmed
(see box, page 20)

1 Peel, core, and roughly chop the apples. Put the peel and cores on a square of cheesecloth and tie up tightly with a long piece of string. Put the apples and water into a preserving pan with the ground ginger, lemon zest, and juice. Tie the cheesecloth bag to the pan handle. Bring to a boil, lower the heat, and simmer, stirring occasionally, for 10 minutes or until the apples are soft. Discard the bag, squeezing it first to extract all the juice.

2 Chop the candied ginger or ginger in syrup; set aside. Add the warmed sugar to the apples, and stir over low heat until the sugar has completely dissolved.

3 Increase the heat and boil the mixture rapidly, without stirring, for 10 minutes or until it reaches setting point. Remove the pan from the heat to test. The candy thermometer should read 220°F. If you do not have a candy thermometer, test for setting with the cold plate test (see page 15).

4 With the pan off the heat, lightly skim off any froth from the surface of the jam, using a long-handled metal spoon, and stir in the chopped ginger. Pour the jam into warmed sterilized jars, to within ¹/₈ inch of the tops. Seal the jars and label.

Makes about 12 cups

Gooseberry and Elderflower Jam

Ingredients

4 lb gooseberries

2¹/₃ cups water

5 large elderflowers

10 cups sugar, warmed
(see box, page 20)

1 Top and tail the gooseberries. Put them with the water into a copper or brass preserving pan (see box, page 26).

2 Cut off and discard the stalks from the elderflowers, and wash the elderflower heads. Put them on a large square of cheesecloth and tie up tightly into a bag with a long piece of string. Tie the cheesecloth bag to the pan handle and bring the fruit and flower mixture to a boil. Lower the heat and simmer, stirring occasionally, for 30–40 minutes or until the fruit is soft. Discard the bag, squeezing it first to extract all of the juice.

3 Add the warmed sugar to the gooseberry mixture, and stir over low heat, until the sugar has completely dissolved.

4 Increase the heat and boil the mixture rapidly, without stirring, for 6–8 minutes or until it reaches setting point. (This jam reaches setting point quickly so start testing early.) Remove the pan from the heat to test. The candy thermometer should read 220°F. If you do not have a candy thermometer, test for setting with the cold plate test (see page 15).

5 With the pan off the heat, lightly skim off any froth from the surface of the jam, using a long-handled metal spoon.

6 Pour the jam into warmed sterilized jars, to within ¹/₈ inch of the tops. Seal the jars and label.

Makes about 8 cups

PRESERVES & CONSERVES

FRUIT PRESERVES, in the narrow sense of the word, are whole fruits or pieces of fruit preserved in a thick syrup – a definition that is accurate but cannot possibly convey the deliciousness of biting into fruits captured from summer's bounty by the subtle use of sugar.

We can enjoy almost any fruits preserved in this simple way – peaches, pears, and strawberries are suitable, so too are exotics like melons and kiwifruit. You can preserve each type of fruit by itself or mix several different ones together for extra flavor and interest. Serve preserves by themselves, as a dessert topping with ice cream, or on a custard or cream pie topped with fresh fruits and whipped cream.

A close culinary cousin of preserves is the conserve, best described as a type of jam. Conserves are often made with two or more fruits, one of which may be a citrus fruit, and usually raisins or nuts are added. They were eaten on their own as a dessert course with a wooden spoon in the late 18th century, but these days they are more often served as spreads, like jams and jellies, or as dessert sauces. They also make fine accompaniments to savory dishes.

MAKING PRESERVES & CONSERVES

❧ Choose the ingredients. All fresh fruits should be picked or purchased when slightly underripe. Dried fruits – prunes, raisins, and apricots – can also be used, provided that they have not been preserved with sulfur dioxide, because this affects the gel. Any dried fruits should be soaked overnight before being used in these recipes. Granulated sugar is the recommended sweetener. Dark brown sugar may be added for additional flavor.

❧ Prepare the fruits. Pick over soft fruits, removing and discarding any moldy or bruised parts. Cut out any blemishes from firmer fruits, such as pears. Wash the fruits, using as little cold water as possible for soft fruits. Pat the fruits dry on paper towels to remove all excess water. Fruits with pits should be halved and pitted, and a few kernels reserved if the recipe calls for it.

❧ For preserves, the chosen fruits are layered with sugar and left to stand overnight. This helps toughen the fruits, enabling them to stay whole, and it also draws out the juices. The next day, the fruits, sugar, and extracted juices are boiled together briefly until a thick syrup is formed. Cool until the fruits remain suspended in the syrup.

❧ The method for making conserves is very similar to jams, but they have a shorter cooking time, so they retain their natural flavor better. The fruits are cooked over low heat until the sugar completely dissolves, then boiled hard to reach a light set.

❧ To test for a light set, drop a little fruit mixture on a cold plate and chill quickly; if the conserve forms a slight wrinkle when pushed with a finger, it is ready to jar.

❧ If adding nuts or alcohol, such as almonds or Grand Marnier, stir them in at the last minute, because cooking destroys their flavor. Pour the preserves or conserves into warmed sterilized jars (see page 11).

How to seal and store

Seal the preserve or conserve as soon as it has been put into the jar. Choose noncorrosive screw-top lids with plastic linings that can be secured tightly. Preserves and conserves do not keep as long as jam, and should be eaten within 3 months. To keep them longer, store them in the refrigerator. They should then last about 6 months.

What can go wrong and why

If the fruits do not stay whole in preserves, they have not been left to stand overnight with the sugar, or they have been cooked too long. If the preserve shrinks in the jar, the seal is faulty or the storage conditions are too warm. Air pockets in the jar are caused if the preserve or conserve is too cool before being poured into the jar. Other problems that occur in jams also apply to preserves and conserves (see page 15).

PRUNE CONSERVE

INGREDIENTS

1½ lb prunes

1½ lb raisins

1½ lb dried currants

4½ cups hot strong tea

2¼ cups packed dark brown
sugar

3–5 whole cloves

juice of 1 lemon

1 cup whole blanched almonds

7 Tb brandy or kirsch

1 Pit the prunes and coarsely chop them. Crack a few of the pits with a hammer and take out the kernels. Discard the rest.

2 Put the kernels into a small bowl and cover with boiling water. Leave for 1 minute, then drain, and transfer to a bowl of cold water. Drain again, then rub off the skins with your fingers.

3 Put the chopped prunes and peeled kernels into a nonmetallic bowl with the raisins and currants. Pour the hot tea over the fruits. Cover and leave to stand overnight.

4 Pour the contents of the bowl into a preserving pan. Stir in all the remaining ingredients, except the almonds, and brandy or kirsch, and put the pan over low heat. Stir with a wooden spoon until the sugar has completely dissolved.

5 Bring the mixture to a boil. Simmer, stirring constantly, for 12 minutes, or until the mixture has thickened. Remove the pan from the heat. Test for a light set (see page 28). Stir in the whole almonds and brandy or kirsch.

6 Pour the conserve into warmed sterilized jars, to within ⅛ inch of the tops. Seal the jars and label.

Makes about 7 cups

PEACH AND MELON PRESERVES

INGREDIENTS

2½ lb peaches

3 lb melon

7 cups sugar

3 Tb lemon juice

pinch of ground ginger

1 cup whole blanched almonds

1 Pit, peel, and roughly chop the peaches. Peel, seed, and chop the melon into large chunks. You should have 2 lb each of chopped peaches and melon.

2 Layer the fruits with the sugar in a large nonmetallic bowl. Cover and leave to stand overnight.

3 Pour the contents of the bowl into a preserving pan and add the lemon juice and ground ginger. Stir the mixture over low heat until the sugar has completely dissolved.

4 Increase the heat and boil the mixture rapidly for 20 minutes or until the mixture has thickened.

5 Remove the pan from the heat and cool slightly until the fruit remains suspended in the syrup. Coarsely chop the almonds and stir into the mixture. Pour the preserve into warmed sterilized jars, to within ⅛ inch of the tops. Seal the jars and label.

Makes about 2 quarts

Above, Peach and Melon Preserves; ***above right****, Prune Conserve*

STRAWBERRY PRESERVES

INGREDIENTS

about 4 quarts (4 lb) small strawberries

9 cups sugar

juice of 1 lemon

Here, whole strawberries are suspended in a sugar syrup.

1 Hull the strawberries. Layer them with the sugar in a nonmetallic bowl. Cover and leave to stand overnight.

2 Pour the contents of the bowl into a preserving pan and add the lemon juice. Bring the mixture to a boil, and simmer for 5 minutes. Return the strawberry mixture to the bowl, cover, and leave for 24 hours.

3 Return the strawberry mixture to the pan and boil rapidly for 20–25 minutes or until the syrup has thickened. Cool slightly until the strawberries remain suspended in the syrup. Pour the preserves into warmed sterilized jars, to within $1/8$ inch of the tops. Seal the jars and label.

COOK'S TIP Strawberry Preserves can be used to make strawberry pavlova – spread a layer of the preserves carefully in a baked meringue shell, and top with whipped cream and fresh strawberries.

Makes about 2 quarts

DRIED APRICOT CONSERVE

INGREDIENTS

4 cups dried apricots

9 cups water

juice of 2 lemons

9 cups sugar, warmed (see box, page 36)

1 1/2 cups blanched almonds

1 Coarsely chop the apricots. Put them into a nonmetallic bowl with the water. Cover and leave to stand overnight.

2 Pour the contents of the bowl into a preserving pan and add the lemon juice. Bring to a boil, and simmer for 15–20 minutes or until the apricots are very soft. Add the warmed sugar. Stir the mixture over low heat until the sugar has completely dissolved.

3 Boil the mixture rapidly, without stirring, for 10–12 minutes or until it has thickened. Remove the pan from the heat. Test for a light set (see page 28). Stir in the blanched almonds and cool slightly.

4 Pour the conserve into warmed sterilized jars, to within $1/8$ inch of the tops. Seal the jars and label.

Makes about 9 cups

GOOSEBERRY AND ALMOND CONSERVE

INGREDIENTS

2 lb gooseberries

3/4 cup lemon juice

1 1/4 cups water

4 cups sugar, warmed (see box, page 36)

1 1/3 cups sliced almonds

1 Top and tail the gooseberries.

2 Combine the gooseberries, lemon juice, and measured water in a copper or brass preserving pan (see box, page 26). Add the warmed sugar, and stir over low heat until the sugar has completely dissolved.

3 Boil the mixture rapidly, stirring occasionally, for 15–20 minutes or until it has thickened. Remove the pan from the heat. Test for a light set (see page 28). Stir in the almonds and cool slightly.

4 Pour the conserve into warmed sterilized jars, to within $1/8$ inch of the tops. Seal the jars and label.

Makes about 1 quart

MELON AND ORANGE PRESERVES

INGREDIENTS

4³/4 lb melon

4 cups sugar

finely grated zest and juice of 1 large orange

juice of 1 lemon

1 Peel and seed the melon and cut into ¹/2 inch cubes. You should have 3 lb of melon after preparing. Layer the melon with the sugar in a nonmetallic bowl. Cover with a cloth and leave to stand overnight.

2 Pour the contents of the bowl into a preserving pan and add the grated orange zest and the orange and lemon juice.

3 Bring the mixture to a boil over a high heat, and boil rapidly for 20–25 minutes or until the syrup has reduced. Cool slightly until the melon remains suspended in the syrup.

4 Pour the preserves into warmed sterilized jars, to within ¹/8 inch of the tops. Seal the jars and label.

Makes about 1 quart

PEAR AND CASHEW CONSERVE

INGREDIENTS

2 lb pears

1¹/4 cups water

juice of 1 lemon

5 cups sugar, warmed (see box, page 36)

3 oz cashews

1 Peel, halve, and core the pears, and cut the flesh into cubes. Put the pears into a saucepan with the water and lemon juice. Bring to boil and simmer for 10 minutes or until the pears are soft and tender.

2 Add the warmed sugar to the fruit mixture and stir over low heat until the sugar has completely dissolved. Boil rapidly for 15–20 minutes, or until the mixture has thickened. Remove the pan from the heat. Test for a light set (see page 28). Chop the cashews and stir them into the conserve. Cool slightly.

3 Pour the conserve into warmed sterilized jars, to within ¹/8 inch of the tops. Seal the jars and label.

Makes about 1 quart

VARIATION
Omit the cashews. Add 1 Tb freshly grated gingerroot to the pears, water, and lemon juice in step 1. When the pear preserve has cooled, stir in 1 Tb rum.

PLUM AND ORANGE CONSERVE

INGREDIENTS

3 lb yellow plums

¹/2 cup drained preserved ginger in syrup

1 cup walnuts

1¹/4 cups water

finely grated zest and juice of 2 large oranges and 2 lemons

9 cups sugar, warmed (see box, page 36)

1 lb raisins

2 Tb brandy

1 Halve and pit the plums. Coarsely chop the drained preserved ginger and the walnuts; set them aside separately.

2 Put the plum halves into a preserving pan with the water and the zest and juice of the oranges and lemons. Bring to a boil and simmer for 30 minutes.

3 Add the warmed sugar to the fruit mixture and stir over low heat until the sugar has completely dissolved. Add the chopped ginger, and the raisins, and return to a boil.

4 Boil rapidly until the mixture has thickened. Remove the pan from the heat. Test for a light set (see page 28). Stir in the walnuts and brandy and cool slightly.

5 Pour the conserve into warmed sterilized jars, to within ¹/8 inch of the tops. Seal the jars and label.

Makes about 11 cups

MARMALADES

IN THE LATE 18th and early 19th centuries, marmalade was a fruit purée that was eaten with a spoon out of an elegant small dish, and it still is served in this way in some parts of the world, such as Latin America and France. But to us, marmalade is the delectable golden wonder we make from citrus fruits and serve on toast at breakfast time.

This preserve is beautiful to look at in jars, and just about any citrus fruits can be used to make it. It can be dark colored, thick, and chunky, or it can be a translucent lemon jelly with thin slices of fruit. In fact, with so many possible combinations of fruits, it can be anything in between.

A citrus preserve is not just for spreading on toast. It can be mixed into puddings and cakes or melted and used with a little liqueur to make a marmalade sauce. In Scotland, marmalade is spread on scones and oatcakes, as well as eaten with certain meats. Make lots and keep your pantry well stocked, as marmalade keeps exceedingly well.

MAKING MARMALADES

❧ Select the ingredients. Bitter Seville oranges give the tangiest, clearest marmalade, but their season of availability is quite short, between December and February. They can be frozen until required, but are best used within a few months because freezing can cause their pectin level to drop slightly. Sweet oranges can also be used but they tend to make a cloudier preserve, and are best used in combination with other fruits, such as limes, lemons, or grapefruit. Granulated sugar is the recommended sweetener. Sometimes the exact amount of sugar is not calculated until after the fruits have been cooked, so make sure you have plenty in stock before you start.

❧ Prepare the fruits. Some citrus fruits have a wax coating that should be removed by pouring boiling water over the fruits, scrubbing, and drying them. The way the fruits are prepared depends on the type of marmalade you are making. There are two basic types – jelly-like, or thick and chunky. Either slice the peel or zest by hand, or save time using a food processor, though this does not give such an even cut. Most of the pectin in citrus fruits, which is needed to set the marmalade, is found in the pith and pits. They should be tied up in a cheesecloth bag and cooked with the rest of the ingredients.

❧ Put the sliced peel, juice, specified amount of water, lemon juice if required, and cheesecloth bag into a preserving pan and simmer for 1 hour or more, until the liquid is reduced by about one-third. This is to soften the peel thoroughly and to extract all of the pectin. Remove the cheesecloth bag, squeezing it well to extract all the excess liquid.

❧ Add warmed sugar (see box, page 36) and stir until dissolved. Boil rapidly until setting point is reached. Test for setting and skim off any froth (see box, page 38). Allow the marmalade to stand for a few minutes off the heat. This helps to ensure that the peel is evenly distributed throughout. As soon as a thin skin forms on the surface, stir the marmalade once and then pour into warmed sterilized jars (see page 11).

How to seal and store
Seal the marmalade as for jams (see page 15), putting the lids on when the marmalade is cold. Label the jars. The marmalade can be used immediately, or it will keep in a cool place for up to 1 year.

What can go wrong and why
If the peel is tough, it has been shredded too coarsely, or cooked for too short a time before the sugar is added. If the peel rises to the surface, the jars were too hot when the marmalade was poured into them.

SEVILLE ORANGE MARMALADE

INGREDIENTS

2 lb Seville oranges

1 large lemon

9 cups water

*9 cups sugar, warmed
(see box, page 36)*

SEVILLE ORANGES The bitter flavor of Seville oranges makes them one of the best citrus fruits for making marmalades. Unfortunately they are only available for a very limited period, but this recipe, or any other requiring Seville oranges, can be made all-year round by substituting sweet oranges for Seville. Just follow this simple formula – for each 1 lb Seville oranges called for, weigh the same amount of sweet oranges. Remove one of the oranges and replace with 1 lemon. The lemon should be dealt with in the same way as the oranges.

1 Cut all the fruit in half and squeeze out the juice, removing and keeping the seeds and excess pith. Strain the juice into a preserving pan. Cut the orange halves in half again and slice thinly across their length. Put the sliced orange peel into the preserving pan.

2 Roughly chop the lemon halves. Put the seeds, pith, and chopped lemon halves on a square of cheesecloth and tie up tightly into a bag with a long piece of string. Tie the cheesecloth bag to the pan handle, so that it rests on the fruit.

3 Pour in the water and bring to a boil. Simmer, stirring occasionally for at least 2 hours or until the peel is very soft. The mixture should have reduced by about one-third.

4 Lift the bag out of the pan and squeeze all the juice back into the pan; discard the bag. Add the warmed sugar and stir over low heat until it has completely dissolved.

5 Increase the heat and boil rapidly, without stirring, for 15–20 minutes or until the marmalade reaches setting point. Test for setting and skim off any scum (see box, page 38).

6 Pour the marmalade into warmed sterilized jars, to within 1/8 inch of the tops. Seal and label.

Makes about 11 cups

MORE MARMALADE FLAVORS

The popularity of Seville Orange Marmalade makes it a good basic recipe that can be varied by adding other flavorings. Here are a few suggestions.

Liqueur Marmalade
A few tablespoons of rum, brandy, or whiskey added to marmalade turn it into a luxurious breakfast preserve. Simply follow the basic recipe above, then stir in the spirit after skimming the marmalade. Allow 1 cup spirit for the whole batch. Let the marmalade stand for a few minutes to ensure the orange peel is evenly distributed throughout. Stir the marmalade once, and continue as directed.

Dark Chunky Marmalade
Follow the basic recipe above, coarsely chopping the orange peel instead of thinly slicing it. When adding the sugar, also stir in 2 Tb molasses.

Seville Orange Marmalade with Almonds
Add 1 cup sliced almonds to the basic recipe above, after skimming the marmalade. Allow the marmalade to stand for a few minutes to ensure the orange peel and nuts are evenly distributed throughout. Stir the marmalade once, and continue as directed.

Brown Sugar Marmalade
For a dark color and rich flavor, substitute 7 cups packed light brown sugar for the sugar in the basic recipe.

DID YOU KNOW?
Marmalade has a long history. Its origins stem from the Middle Ages, when it was made with quinces cooked in honey, wine, and spices and called "marmelade." The word is derived from *marmelada*, Portuguese for quince. It was during the 17th century that recipes for a kind of orange marmalade appeared.

THREE-FRUIT MARMALADE

Wonderfully tangy, this marmalade can be made year-round because it does not need seasonal Seville oranges. Don't save it just for breakfast – try using it as a glossy glaze for brushing over duck, baked ham, and chicken breasts.

INGREDIENTS

2 grapefruit

2 large oranges

4 lemons

15 cups water

5 1/2 cups sugar, warmed
(see box, page 36)

Makes about 13 1/2 cups

1 ◀ Cut all of the fruit in half and squeeze out the juice. Strain the juice into a preserving pan. Remove the seeds and pulp from the skins and put them on a square of cheesecloth. Tie up tightly into a bag with a long piece of string.

2 ▶ Cut the orange and lemon halves in half again and slice thinly across their length. Cut each grapefruit half into quarters and slice in the same way. Put all the sliced fruit peel into the pan.

3 ◀ Tie the muslin bag to the pan handle so that it rests on top of the fruit peel. Pour in the water and bring to a boil. Lower the heat and simmer, stirring occasionally, for 30–40 minutes or until the peel is very soft. The mixture should have reduced by about one-third.

4 ◀ Lift the bag out of the pan and squeeze all the juice back into the pan. Discard the bag. Add the warmed sugar and stir over low heat until it has completely dissolved.

5 ▲ Increase the heat and boil rapidly, without stirring, for 20–25 minutes or until the marmalade reaches setting point. Remove from the heat to test. The candy thermometer should read 220°F. Alternatively, test for setting with the cold plate test (see box, below).

COLD PLATE TEST

Also known as the saucer test. Put a small spoonful of marmalade on a cold plate and chill quickly in the refrigerator. If the marmalade has boiled sufficiently, a thin skin will form on the surface and it should wrinkle when pushed with a finger. It is now at setting point.

6 ▲ With the pan off the heat, skim off any froth. Leave to cool for a few minutes until a very thin skin forms. This helps ensure that the peel is evenly distributed.

7 Pour the marmalade into warmed sterilized jars, to within ⅛ inch of the tops. Seal the jars and label.

BREAKFAST TREAT
Start the day with the refreshing taste of homemade marmalade.

*F*INE-SHRED MARMALADE

INGREDIENTS

2 lb Seville oranges
(see box, page 33)

1 lemon

10 cups water

sugar

WARMING SUGAR In some recipes, the amount of sugar required is calculated according to the amount of strained juice you have after the fruit is cooked. It is therefore difficult to be specific with an exact amount of sugar in the ingredients list, so make sure you have a good supply before you start. After weighing out the sugar, it can be warmed so that it dissolves more quickly in the juice. Put the oven on its lowest setting, and put the sugar in an ovenproof bowl. Warm the sugar in the oven for about 15 minutes.

1 Pare the zest from the oranges and lemon and slice it into thin strips. Put the sliced zest in a stainless steel pan with $1^{1}/_{4}$ cups of the water, making sure the zest is covered, and bring to a boil. Simmer, stirring occasionally, for 1 hour or until the zest is very soft. Drain and reserve both zest and water.

2 Chop the fruit and put into a preserving pan with all the seeds and the remaining $8^{3}/_{4}$ cups water. Bring to a boil, lower the heat, and simmer, stirring occasionally, for about 1 hour. The mixture should have reduced by about one-third. Add the water reserved from cooking the zest.

3 Strain the pulp through a scalded jelly bag (see box, page 41). (For a clear marmalade, allow the juice to drip through without pressing it.) Measure the strained juice. For each $2^{1}/_{3}$ cups juice, measure $2^{1}/_{4}$ cups sugar. Warm the sugar (see box, left). Pour the juice into the pan, add the sugar and stir. Stir over a low heat until the sugar has completely dissolved.

4 Add the reserved zest and bring to a boil. Boil rapidly, without stirring, for 10–12 minutes or until it reaches setting point. Test for set and skim off any froth (see box, page 38). Pour the marmalade into warmed sterilized jars, to within $1/_8$ inch of the tops. Seal the jars and label.

Makes about 2 quarts

*T*ANGERINE MARMALADE

INGREDIENTS

2 lb tangerines

1 grapefruit

2 lemons

12 cups water

8 cups sugar, warmed
(see box, above)

1 Peel the tangerines and slice the peel into thin strips. Put the strips on a square of cheesecloth and tie up tightly into a bag with a long piece of string. Chop the tangerine flesh, removing and keeping the seeds. Put the flesh into a preserving pan.

2 Pare the zest from the grapefruit and lemons and slice it into thin strips, removing and keeping any excess pith. Put the sliced zest in the pan. Chop the grapefruit and lemon flesh and add to the pan, removing and keeping the seeds. Put all the seeds and pith on a square of cheesecloth and tie up tightly into a bag with a long piece of string. Tie both cheesecloth bags to the pan handle, so that they rest on the fruit.

3 Pour in the water and bring to a boil. Simmer, stirring occasionally, for 45 minutes or until the zest is very soft. The mixture should have reduced by about one-third. Lift the bag of seeds and pith out of the pan and squeeze all the juice back into the pan; discard the bag. Lift out the bag of tangerine peel and empty it into the pan. Add the warmed sugar and stir over low heat until it has completely dissolved.

4 Increase the heat and boil the mixture rapidly, without stirring, for 15–20 minutes or until the marmalade reaches setting point. Test for set and skim off any froth (see box, page 38). Pour the marmalade into warmed sterilized jars, to within $1/_8$ inch of the tops. Seal the jars and label.

Makes about 2 quarts

PINK GRAPEFRUIT MARMALADE

INGREDIENTS

2 lemons

2 pink grapefruit

9 cups water

*9 cups sugar, warmed
(see box, page 36)*

1 Pare the zest from the lemons and slice it into thin strips. Put the strips into a preserving pan. Cut the lemons and grapefruit in half and squeeze out the juice, removing and keeping the seeds. Add the juice to the lemon zest in the pan.

2 Roughly chop the lemon halves and put with the seeds on a square of cheesecloth. Tie up tightly into a bag with a long piece of string. Cut the grapefruit halves into 4 pieces and slice thinly across their length. Add to the pan. Tie the cheesecloth bag to the pan handle, so that it rests on the fruit.

3 Pour in the water and bring to a boil. Lower the heat and simmer, stirring occasionally, for 45 minutes or until the skins are soft. The mixture should have reduced by about one-third.

4 Lift the bag out of the pan and squeeze all the juice back into the pan. Discard the bag. Add the warmed sugar to the mixture and stir over low heat until it has completely dissolved. Increase the heat and boil rapidly, without stirring, for 10–12 minutes or until the marmalade reaches setting point. Test for set and skim off any froth (see box, page 38). Pour the marmalade into warmed sterilized jars, to within ⅛ inch of the tops. Seal the jars and label.

Makes about 7 cups

LEMON AND LIME MARMALADE

INGREDIENTS

4 medium lemons

4 limes

9 cups water

*9 cups sugar,
warmed
(see box, page 36)*

1 Pare the zest from the lemons and slice it into thin strips. Cut the pith off the lemons, roughly chop it, and set it aside. Roughly chop the flesh, keeping the seeds and any juice.

2 Cut the limes in half and squeeze out the juice, removing and keeping the seeds and excess pith. Cut the lime halves in half again and slice thinly across their length.

3 Put all the seeds and pith on a square of cheesecloth and tie up tightly into a bag with a long piece of string.

4 Put all the flesh, juice, lime skins, and lemon zest into a preserving pan. Tie the cheesecloth bag to the pan handle, so that it rests on the fruit. Pour in the water and bring to a boil. Simmer, stirring occasionally, for 1½ hours or until the skins are very soft. The mixture should have reduced by about one-third.

5 Lift the bag out of the pan and squeeze all the juice back into the pan. Discard the bag. Add the warmed sugar and stir over low heat until it has completely dissolved. Increase the heat and boil rapidly, without stirring, for 8–10 minutes or until the marmalade reaches setting point. Test for set and skim off any froth (see box, page 38). Pour the marmalade into warmed sterilized jars, to within ⅛ inch of the tops. Seal the jars and label.

Makes about 2 quarts

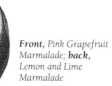

Front, *Pink Grapefruit Marmalade;* **back,** *Lemon and Lime Marmalade*

SWEET ORANGE MARMALADE

INGREDIENTS

2 lb sweet oranges.

2 Seville oranges
(see box, page 33)

1 lemon

9 cups water

9 cups sugar, warmed
(see box, page 36)

This marmalade blends sweet oranges with the more tart Seville oranges, to give a delicious and refreshing taste.

1 Cut all the fruit in half and squeeze out the juice, removing and keeping the seeds and any excess pith. Pour the juice into a preserving pan. Put the seeds and pith on a square of cheesecloth and tie up tightly into a bag with a piece of string.

2 Cut the orange halves in half again and slice them thinly across their length. Discard the lemon peel.

3 Put all the sliced peel in the pan. Tie the cheesecloth bag to the pan handle, so that it rests on the fruit. Pour in the water and bring to a boil. Simmer, stirring occasionally, for $1\frac{1}{2}$–2 hours or until the skins are very soft. The mixture should have reduced by about one-third.

4 Lift the bag out of the pan and squeeze out all the juice back into the pan. Discard the bag.

5 Add the warmed sugar and stir over low heat until it has completely dissolved.

6 Increase the heat and boil the mixture rapidly, without stirring, for 15–20 minutes or until it reaches setting point. Test for set and skim off any froth (see box, left). Pour the marmalade into warmed sterilized jars, to within $\frac{1}{8}$ inch of the tops. Seal the jars and label.

Makes about 9 cups

TESTING FOR SET AND SKIMMING MARMALADES

Remove the pan from the heat. If using a sugar thermometer, it should read 220°F. If you do not have a thermometer, use the cold plate test: drop a little of the marmalade on a cold plate and chill quickly in the refrigerator. If it forms a skin and wrinkles when pushed with a finger, it should be ready. Lightly skim off any froth from the pan of marmalade, then leave to cool for a few minutes until a very thin skin forms. This helps to ensure that the peel is evenly distributed through the marmalade.

QUICK CHUNKY MARMALADE

INGREDIENTS

6 Seville oranges
(see box, page 33)

2 large sweet oranges

2 large lemons

15 cups water

13 cups sugar, warmed
(see box, page 36)

1 Cut all the fruit in half and squeeze out the juice, removing and keeping the seeds and any excess pith. Pour the juice into a preserving pan. Put the seeds and pith on a square of cheesecloth and tie up tightly with a long piece of string.

2 Cut the orange and lemon halves into smaller pieces and chop well in small batches, in a food processor, adding a little of the water, if necessary.

3 Put the processed fruit into the pan. Tie the cheesecloth bag to the pan handle, so that it rests on the fruit. Pour in the water and bring to a boil. Simmer, stirring occasionally, for $1\frac{1}{2}$–2 hours or until the skins are very soft. The mixture should have reduced by about one-third.

4 Lift the bag out of the pan and squeeze all the juice back into the pan. Discard the bag. Add the warmed sugar and stir over low heat until it has completely dissolved. Increase the heat and boil rapidly, without stirring, for 15 minutes or until it reaches setting point. Test for set and skim off any froth (see box, above). Pour the marmalade into warmed sterilized jars, to within $\frac{1}{8}$ inch of the tops. Seal the jars and label.

Makes about 11 cups

COOK'S TIP

Chopping citrus fruits in a food processor is much quicker than by hand – although it does give a coarser cut. A blender can also be used for chopping, but the result is more like a paste.

*L*EMON MARMALADE

INGREDIENTS

9 large lemons

15 cups water

*sugar, warmed
(see box, page 36)*

1 Pare the zest from the lemons, and slice it into thin strips. Roughly chop the flesh, keeping the seeds and any juice. Put the seeds on a square of cheesecloth and tie up tightly into a bag with a long piece of string.

2 Put the chopped flesh and any juice with the sliced zest in a preserving pan. Tie the cheesecloth bag to the pan handle, so that it rests on the fruit. Pour in the water and bring to a boil. Lower the heat and simmer, stirring occasionally, for 1–1½ hours, or until the zest is very soft. The mixture should have reduced by about one-third.

3 Lift the bag out of the pan and squeeze out all the juice back into the pan. Discard the bag. Measure the juice. For each 2 cups juice, measure 2 cups sugar. Warm the sugar (see box, page 36). Pour the juice back into the pan, add the sugar, and stir over a low heat until it has completely dissolved. Boil rapidly, without stirring, for 15 minutes or until the marmalade reaches setting point. Test for set and skim off any froth (see box, page 38). Pour into warmed sterilized jars, to within ⅛ inch of the tops. Seal the jars and label.

Makes about 2 quarts

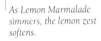

As Lemon Marmalade simmers, the lemon zest softens.

*G*RAPEFRUIT AND GINGER MARMALADE

INGREDIENTS

3 large grapefruit

3 lemons

15 cups water

1 inch piece of fresh gingerroot, peeled

*11 cups sugar, warmed
(see box, page 36)*

⅔ cup chopped candied ginger

1 Peel the fruit. Finely slice the grapefruit peel and put it into a preserving pan. Chop the flesh of both fruits and add to the pan. Chop the lemon peel and put it on a square of cheesecloth, together with the seeds. Tie the bag to the pan handle, so that it rests on the fruit. Pour in the water. Peel the gingerroot, and add to the pan.

2 Bring to a boil and simmer, stirring occasionally, for 1½ hours, or until the skins are very soft. The mixture should have reduced by about one-third.

3 Remove and discard the gingerroot. Lift the bag out of the pan and squeeze all the juice back into the pan. Discard the bag. Add the warmed sugar to the mixture and stir over low heat until the sugar has completely dissolved.

4 Increase the heat and boil rapidly, without stirring, for 15 minutes or until the marmalade reaches setting point. Test for set and skim off any froth (see box, page 38). Pour the marmalade into warmed sterilized jars, to within ⅛ inch of the tops. Stir in the candied ginger. Seal the jars and label.

Makes about 11 cups

$\mathcal{J}$ELLIES

BRIGHTLY COLORED, delicately flavored, firm yet quivering gently when released from its jar, the ideal jelly is a thing of beauty and a joy to eat. It is wonderful on toast, bread and butter and scones, and in peanut butter sandwiches. It also makes a deliciously sweet counterpoint to savory foods, such as roast poultry, pork, and game. And unlike poor Meg's jelly in Louisa May Alcott's book, *Little Women*, today's jellies do gel if the simple rules for making them are respected.

Jellies are a marvelous challenge to the imaginative cook. Peaches, cherries, and cranberries are just a few of the suitable fruits. Apples, with their high levels of pectin which help achieve set, make wonderful companions for other fruits. Apple and Orange Jelly and Apple and Chili Jelly both testify to the versatility of the accommodating apple when making jellies. The addition of a few rose or geranium leaves can lift jellies out of the ordinary, and herbs and spices can also play an interesting role. The possibilities are infinite. Don't hestitate to experiment.

$\mathcal{M}$AKING JELLIES

❦ Choose your ingredients. Select ripe fruits, but not overripe, with a high pectin content. Apples (including crab apples), currants, berries, and citrus fruits all make good jellies. Granulated sugar is the recommended sweetener. Make sure you have plenty in stock, because the exact amount required is not calculated until after the fruits have been cooked.

❦ Prepare the fruits. Pick over soft fruits, removing and discarding any moldy or bruised parts. Wash and dry the fruits. Any peel, seeds, and cores all go in the preserving pan with the flesh. Add water and simmer until the fruits are soft and pulpy.

❦ Strain the pulp through a scalded jelly bag (see box, page 41). Timing varies, depending on the fruits used. Leave to strain for a few hours or overnight, but not more than 24 hours or the fruits will start to oxidize.

❦ Measure the juice and pour into a clean preserving pan with the sugar. The amount of sugar used will depend upon the pectin content of the juice, but in general, $2\frac{1}{4}$ cups sugar is required for each $2\frac{1}{3}$ cups juice. Warm the sugar before adding it to the preserving pan (see box, page 44). Stir over low heat until the sugar has completely dissolved. Boil rapidly for 10 minutes, or until setting point is reached. When the jelly nears setting point, lower the heat slightly to reduce the number of bubbles. Remove the pan from the heat to test. Test for setting and skim off any froth (see box, page 46).

❦ Pour the jelly into warmed sterilized jars (see page 11). Tilt the jars and pour the jelly down the sides of the jars to eliminate air pockets. Work as quickly as possible, because the jelly may start to set in the pan, and this will spoil the consistency of the finished jelly.

How to seal and store
Seal and store the jellies in the same way as for jams (see page 15). Do not move the jelly until it is completely cold and set.

What can go wrong and why
If the jelly remains runny after it is cold, it can be returned to the pan for additional boiling. Jellies will be cloudy if the fruits are not clean, if the jelly bag has too coarse a mesh, or if the bag is squeezed during straining. Air pockets will form in the jelly if it is too cool before being poured into jars, or poured into jars too slowly.

RED FRUIT JELLY WITH PORT

INGREDIENTS

2 lb red currants

2 quarts raspberries

1³/₄ cups water

sugar

¹/₄ cup port

USING A JELLY BAG Jelly bags need to be supported while the juice is straining. One way of doing this is to thread a broomstick through the straps of the jelly bag, then rest each end of the broom on a chair. Place a large nonmetallic bowl underneath before filling the jelly bag and let the juice drip undisturbed. Resist the temptation to accelerate the process by squeezing the bag, because this will result in a cloudy jelly. Leave to drip until there is only a little liquid dripping from the bag.

1 Put the red currants and raspberries into a preserving pan with the water. Bring to a boil, and simmer for 15–20 minutes or until the fruits are very soft and pulpy.

2 While the fruits are cooking, prepare the jelly bag for straining the fruits. Scald it by evenly pouring through boiling water, squeeze it well, then use as directed (see box, left). Pour the fruit pulp into the jelly bag and leave to strain for a few hours or overnight, but not more than 24 hours.

3 Measure the strained juice. For each 2¹/₃ cups juice, measure 2¹/₄ cups sugar. Pour the juice into a clean preserving pan. Warm the sugar (see box, page 44), and add it to the juice. Stir over low heat until the sugar has completely dissolved.

4 Increase the heat and boil the mixture rapidly, without stirring, for 9–10 minutes or until it reaches setting point. Test for setting and skim off any froth (see box, page 46). Stir in the port.

5 Immediately pour the jelly into warmed sterilized jars, tilting them slightly to prevent air pockets from forming. Seal the jars and label.

Makes about 1 quart

MINT AND APPLE JELLY

INGREDIENTS

3 lb cooking apples

2¹/₃ cups water

1¹/₄ cups cider vinegar

8 oz fresh mint

sugar

2–3 drops of green food coloring (optional)

1 Chop the apples without peeling or coring them. Put them into a preserving pan with the water and vinegar. Strip the mint leaves from their stalks and set aside. Add the stalks to the pan. Bring the mixture to a boil, and simmer for about 40 minutes or until the apples are very soft and pulpy.

2 While the apples are cooking, prepare the jelly bag for straining the fruit. Scald it by evenly pouring through boiling water, squeeze it well, then use as directed (see box, above). Pour the fruit pulp into the jelly bag and leave to strain for a few hours or overnight, but not more than 24 hours.

3 Measure the strained juice. For each 2¹/₃ cups juice, measure 2¹/₄ cups sugar. Pour the juice into a clean preserving pan. Warm the sugar (see box, page 44) and add it to the juice. Stir over low heat until the sugar has completely dissolved. Tie half of the mint leaves in a cheesecloth bag and add to the jelly mixture. Increase the heat and boil the mixture rapidly, without stirring, for 15 minutes or until it reaches setting point. Test for setting and skim off any froth (see box, page 46).

4 Remove the cheesecloth bag, squeezing all the juice back into the pan; discard the bag. Chop the remaining mint leaves. Stir in the freshly chopped mint and green food coloring, if using.

5 Immediately pour the jelly into warmed sterilized jars, tilting them slightly to prevent air pockets from forming. Seal the jars and label.

Makes about 2 cups

VARIATIONS
Other herb and apple jellies can be made using the same method as for mint. Parsley, sage, rosemary, and thyme are all equally good.

Jelly-making equipment

CRANBERRY AND APPLE JELLY

Ruby-red cranberries are popular for festive holiday occasions. In this recipe they are teamed up with apples, creating a tart, garnet-colored jelly. Cranberry and Apple Jelly is a delicious accompaniment to roast pork, cold meats, and poultry – especially roast turkey.

INGREDIENTS

3 lb cooking apples

2 lb fresh cranberries

4¹/₂ cups water

about 4 cups sugar

Makes about 5 cups

1 ◀ Cut out any bruised or damaged parts from the apples, then coarsely chop the apples without peeling or coring them.

2 ▼ Put the apples into a preserving pan with the fresh cranberries.

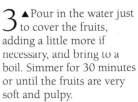

3 ▲ Pour in the water just to cover the fruits, adding a little more if necessary, and bring to a boil. Simmer for 30 minutes or until the fruits are very soft and pulpy.

4 While the apples and cranberries are cooking, prepare a jelly bag for straining the fruits. Scald the jelly bag by pouring boiling water evenly through it, squeeze it well, then suspend the bag over a large nonmetallic bowl.

5 ▶ Ladle the fruit pulp into the jelly bag and leave to strain for a few hours, or overnight, but not more than 24 hours. Make sure that the jelly bag is not squeezed or shaken while the pulp is straining, or the jelly will be cloudy.

6 ▲ Measure the strained juice. For each 2 1/3 cups juice, measure 2 cups sugar. Pour the juice into a clean preserving pan. Warm the sugar and add it to the juice. Stir over low heat, with a wooden spoon, until the sugar has completely dissolved.

7 ▲ Increase the heat and boil the mixture rapidly, without stirring, for 10–12 minutes or until it reaches setting point. Remove the pan from the heat to test for setting, and skim off any scum (see box, page 46). Pour the jelly into warmed sterilized jars, tilting them slightly to prevent air pockets from forming. Seal the jars and label.

43

Apple and Orange Jelly

INGREDIENTS

2¹/₂ lb cooking apples

3 oranges

4¹/₂ cups water

sugar

WARMING SUGAR In these jelly recipes the amount of sugar required is calculated according to the amount of strained juice you have after the fruit is cooked. It is therefore difficult to be specific with an exact amount of sugar in the ingredients list, so make sure you have a good supply before you start. After weighing the sugar, it can be warmed so it dissolves quicker in the juice. Put the oven on its lowest setting, and put the sugar into an ovenproof bowl. Warm the sugar for about 15 minutes.

1 Peel, core, and chop the apples, reserving the cores and seeds. Chop the unpeeled oranges and remove the seeds. Put the apple cores and apple and orange seeds on a square of cheesecloth and tie up tightly with a long piece of string.

2 Put the fruits with the water into a preserving pan and bring to a boil. Simmer for 50 minutes or until the fruits are soft and pulpy.

3 While the apples and oranges are cooking, prepare the jelly bag for straining the fruits. Scald it by evenly pouring through boiling water, squeeze it well, then use as directed (see box, page 41). Remove the muslin bag from the fruit pulp and discard. Pour the fruit pulp into the jelly bag and leave to strain for a few hours or overnight, but not more than 24 hours.

4 Measure the strained juice. For each 2¹/₃ cups juice, measure 2¹/₄ cups sugar. Pour the juice into a clean preserving pan. Warm the sugar (see box, left), and add it to the juice. Stir over low heat until the sugar has completely dissolved.

5 Increase the heat and boil the mixture rapidly, without stirring, for 10–12 minutes or until it reaches setting point. Test for setting and skim off any froth (see box, page 46).

6 Pour the jelly into warmed sterilized jars, tilting them slightly to prevent air pockets from forming. Seal the jars and label.

Makes about 5 cups

Mixed Fruit Jelly

INGREDIENTS

1 lb cooking apples

4 large oranges

1 lemon

7 cups water

1 quart strawberries

sugar

1 Coarsely chop the apples, oranges, and lemons, without peeling, seeding, or coring them. Put them into a preserving pan with the water. Bring to a boil, and simmer for 40–45 minutes or until the fruits are very soft and pulpy.

2 Hull and halve the strawberries and add them to the pan. Bring the mixture back to a boil, and simmer for 5 minutes or until the strawberries are very soft.

3 While the strawberries are cooking, prepare the jelly bag for straining the fruits. Scald it by evenly pouring through boiling water, squeeze it well, then use as directed (see box, page 41). Pour the fruit pulp into the jelly bag and leave to strain for a few hours or overnight, but not more than 24 hours.

4 Measure the strained juice. For each 2¹/₃ cups juice, measure 2¹/₄ cups sugar. Pour the juice into a clean preserving pan. Warm the sugar (see box, above), and add it to the juice. Stir over low heat until the sugar has completely dissolved.

5 Increase the heat and boil the mixture rapidly, without stirring, for 30–35 minutes or until it reaches setting point. Test for setting and skim off any froth (see box, page 46). Immediately pour the jelly into warmed sterilized jars, tilting them slightly to prevent air pockets from forming. Seal the jars and label.

Makes about 4¹/₄ cups

APPLE AND CHILI JELLY

INGREDIENTS

3 lb cooking apples

2 1/3 cups water

1 1/4 cups cider vinegar

4 oz fresh green chilies

sugar

2–3 drops of green food coloring (optional)

1 Chop the apples without peeling or coring them. Put them into a preserving pan with the water and vinegar.

2 Trim the chilies and cut in half lengthwise. Remove and discard the seeds. Add the chilies to the pan with the apples.

3 Bring the mixture to a boil, and simmer for 20–25 minutes or until the fruit is very soft and pulpy.

4 While the apples and chilies are cooking, prepare the jelly bag for straining the fruits. Scald it by evenly pouring through boiling water, squeeze it well, then use as directed (see box, page 41). Pour the pulp into the jelly bag and leave to strain for a few hours or overnight, but not more than 24 hours.

5 Measure the strained juice. For each 2 1/3 cups juice, measure 2 1/4 cups sugar. Pour the juice into a clean preserving pan. Warm the sugar (see box, page 44), and add it to the juice. Stir over low heat until the sugar has completely dissolved.

6 Increase the heat, and boil the mixture rapidly, without stirring, for 8–10 minutes, or until it reaches setting point. Test for setting and skim off any froth (see box, page 46).

7 Stir in the food coloring, if using. Immediately pour the jelly into warmed sterilized jars, tilting them slightly to prevent air pockets from forming. Seal the jars and label.

Makes about 1 1/2 cups

COOK'S TIP

Chilies should be prepared with care. Wear rubber gloves when handling them, as it can be painful if any chili gets on the skin, eyes or nose. Afterwards, wash all surfaces and equipment that have come in contact with the chilies.

GRAPE JELLY

INGREDIENTS

3 lb green grapes

juice of 2 lemons

2 1/3 cups water

sugar

1 Coarsely chop the grapes and put them into a preserving pan with the lemon juice and water. Bring to a boil, and simmer for 30 minutes or until the grapes are very soft and pulpy.

2 While the grapes are cooking, prepare the jelly bag for straining the grapes. Scald it by evenly pouring through boiling water, squeeze it well, then use as directed (see box, page 41). Pour the grape pulp into the jelly bag and leave to strain for a few hours or overnight, but not more than 24 hours.

3 Measure the strained juice. For each 2 1/3 cups juice, measure 2 1/4 cups sugar. Pour the juice into a clean preserving pan. Warm the sugar (see box, page 44), and add it to the juice. Stir over low heat until the sugar has completely dissolved.

4 Increase the heat and boil the mixture rapidly, without stirring, for 12 minutes or until it reaches setting point. Test for setting and skim off any froth (see box, page 46).

5 Immediately pour the jelly into warmed sterilized jars, tilting them slightly to prevent air pockets from forming. Seal the jars and label.

Makes about 2 cups

CHAMELEON
Despite using green grapes, Grape Jelly has a pink hue.

BLACKBERRY JELLY

INGREDIENTS

5 lb blackberries

juice of 2 lemons

3²/₃ cups water

sugar

1 Put the blackberries into a preserving pan with the lemon juice and water. Bring to a boil, and simmer for 30 minutes or until the fruit is very soft and pulpy.

2 While the blackberries are cooking, prepare the jelly bag for straining the fruit. Scald it by evenly pouring boiling water through, squeeze it well, then use as directed (see box, page 41). Pour the fruit pulp into the jelly bag and leave the blackberry pulp to strain for a few hours or overnight, but not more than 24 hours.

3 Measure the strained juice. For each 2¹/₃ cups juice, measure 2¹/₄ cups sugar. Pour the juice into a clean preserving pan. Warm the sugar (see box, page 44) and add it to the juice. Stir over low heat, with a wooden spoon, until the sugar has completely dissolved.

4 Increase the heat and boil the mixture rapidly, without stirring, for 9–10 minutes or until it reaches setting point. Test for setting and skim off any froth (see box, left).

5 Take the pan off the heat. Immediately pour the jelly into warmed sterilized jars, tilting them slightly to prevent air pockets from forming. Seal the jars and label.

Makes about 1 quart

TESTING FOR SETTING AND SKIMMING JELLIES

Remove the pan from the heat. The best way to test is with a candy thermometer, which should read 220°F when setting point is reached. If you do not have a thermometer, use the cold plate test: drop a little of the jelly on a cold plate and chill quickly in the refrigerator. If it forms a skin and wrinkles when pushed with a finger, it should be ready. Lightly skim off any froth from the surface of the jelly, using a long-handled metal spoon.

CRAB APPLE JELLY

INGREDIENTS

6 lb crab apples

juice of 2 lemons

7 cups water

5 whole cloves

sugar

1 Coarsely chop the crab apples without peeling or coring them. Put them into a preserving pan with the lemon juice, water, and cloves. Bring the mixture to a boil, and simmer for 40 minutes or until the fruit is very soft and pulpy.

2 While the apples are cooking, prepare the jelly bag for straining the fruit. Scald it by evenly pouring through boiling water, squeeze it well, then use as directed (see box, page 41). Pour the fruit pulp into the jelly bag and leave to strain for a few hours or overnight, but not more than 24 hours.

3 Measure the strained juice. For each 2¹/₃ cups juice, measure 2¹/₄ cups sugar. Pour the juice into a clean preserving pan. Warm the sugar (see box, page 44), and add it to the juice. Stir over low heat until the sugar has completely dissolved.

4 Increase the heat and boil the mixture rapidly, without stirring, for 9–10 minutes or until it reaches setting point. Test for setting and skim off any froth (see box, above).

5 Immediately pour the jelly into warmed sterilized jars, tilting them slightly to prevent air pockets from forming. Seal the jars and label.

Makes about 3¹/₂ cups

FRUIT BUTTERS & SPREADS

A GLUT OF sun-ripened fruits, available in the shops at bargain prices, means it is time to make fruit butters and spreads. They are so easy to prepare and require no special skill or equipment except a good wooden spoon for stirring. The bittersweet flavor and smooth spreadable texture of butters make them an ideal substitute for ordinary butter on bread, toast, scones, and unfrosted cake. The fruit spreads are more substantial; and they look good set in shapely molds, then turned out and sliced, cubed, or cut into wedges.

In England they are aptly called fruit cheeses; elsewhere they are sometimes called pastes (*pâtes* in France). Whatever the name, they are popular around the world. In the south of France and Brazil, they may be served as sweetmeats or together with fresh cheeses. Guavas, quinces, mangoes, and pineapples are all used for making fruit cheeses in Mexico, where they are often eaten with cream cheese and crackers. Closer to home, we are most likely to use them to embellish baked goods, and thus in this book they are labeled simply spreads.

MAKING FRUIT BUTTERS & SPREADS

❧ Choose the ingredients. Most fruits can be used, but sharply flavored ones, such as plums, quinces, damsons, and currants work best. Spices can be added. White sugar is the recommended sweetener.

❧ Wash, pit or hull, and chop the fruits as necessary, removing any moldy or bruised parts. Put the fruits into a preserving pan. Barely cover the fruits with water and bring to a boil, then simmer, stirring occasionally, over low heat, until the fruits are soft and pulpy and there is no excess liquid. Sieve or blend the fruits to a purée.

❧ Measure the fruit pulp. For fruit butters, measure 1–1¼ cups sugar for each 1 cup pulp. For fruit spreads, measure 1⅔ cups sugar for each 1 cup pulp. Warm the sugar (see box, page 44). Return the pulp to the pan with the sugar, add spices if using, and stir over low heat until the sugar has completely dissolved.

❧ Bring to a boil, and simmer 30–45 minutes for butters and 45–60 minutes for spreads, stirring frequently to prevent them from burning. The butter is ready when a spoonful placed on a saucer does not exude any liquid. The spread is ready when a spoon drawn across the bottom of the pan leaves a clean line.

❧ Spoon the butters into sterilized jars (see page 11), and seal. For spreads, pour the mixture into molds that they can be turned out for slicing. Brush the molds with a little glycerine so the spreads will slip out easily.

How to seal and store

Screw-top lids and two-piece screwband lids are the best choice for sealing fruit butters, because butters have a tendency to dry out, and need an airtight seal. Butters, which have a thick spreading consistency, do not keep quite as well as jams and should be used up within 3 months. If the spreads are in molds, cover them as you would jams with melted paraffin wax. Leave the wax to cool and cover the jars with a protective lid (see page 15). Fruit spreads have a higher sugar content than butters and will keep for up to 1 year.

What can go wrong and why

If the butter starts to ferment, this could be a result either of too short a cooking time or of too little sugar. The mixtures may crystallize if the excess water has not evaporated before adding the sugar.

STRAWBERRY-PEAR BUTTER

The flavors of summer and autumn blend together in this thick, creamy preserve. Serve it in summer spooned onto freshly made pancakes with sliced strawberries and cream, or on a winter's afternoon, spread on hot buttered scones or toast. Small jars of this fruit butter also make pretty gifts for special occasions.

INGREDIENTS

4 lb pears

4 cups strawberries

1¹/₄ cups water

¹/₂ tsp ground cinnamon

sugar

Makes about 3 ¹/₂ cups

1 ▼ Peel the pears, cut into quarters, and remove and discard the cores. Chop the pears finely. Hull the strawberries and cut them into quarters.

2 Put the pears and strawberries into a preserving pan. Add the water and ground cinnamon and bring to a boil. Simmer, stirring, for 1–1¹/₄ hours or until the fruits are very soft. The mixture should be thick and pulpy, and all of the excess liquid should have evaporated.

3 ◄ With a wooden spoon, press the fruit mixture through a plastic sieve set over a nonmetallic bowl. Measure the sieved pulp. For each 2 cups pulp, measure 1¹/₂ cups sugar. Warm the sugar (see box, page 44).

4 Return the pulp to the pan, and add the sugar. Stir the mixture over low heat, with a wooden spoon, until the sugar has completely dissolved.

5 ▼ Simmer over low heat, stirring frequently, until the butter thickens to resemble applesauce. This will take 15–20 minutes. The butter is ready to jar when a spoonful placed on a saucer does not exude any liquid.

6 Remove the pan from the heat. Spoon the butter into warmed sterilized jars, to within ¹/₈ inch of the tops. Seal the jars and label.

PEACH BUTTER

INGREDIENTS

2 lb ripe peaches

2 cups water

sugar

1 Drop the peaches into boiling water for 1–2 minutes, depending on their ripeness, then transfer to a bowl of ice water. Drain the peaches when cool.

2 Halve the peaches, discard the pits, peel, and coarsely chop the flesh. Put the flesh into a saucepan with the measured water. Simmer, stirring occasionally, for 20 minutes or until very soft. Press through a plastic sieve set over a nonmetallic bowl.

3 Measure the sieved pulp. For each 1 cup pulp, measure $^1/_2$ cup sugar. Warm the sugar (see box, page 44). Return the pulp to the pan, add the sugar, and simmer over low heat, stirring frequently, for 30 minutes, or until the butter thickens to resemble applesauce.

4 Spoon the butter into warmed sterilized jars, seal, and label.

Makes about 2$^1/_4$ cups

CRANBERRY BUTTER

INGREDIENTS

3 lb fresh cranberries

1 cup water

sugar

1 Put the fruit into a preserving pan with the measured water and bring to a boil. Simmer, stirring occasionally, for 35–40 minutes, or until the cranberries are very soft. Press the cranberries through a plastic sieve set over a nonmetallic bowl.

2 Measure the sieved pulp. For each 2 cups pulp, measure 1$^1/_2$ cups sugar. Warm the sugar (see box, page 44). Return the pulp to the pan, add the sugar, and stir over low heat until the sugar has completely dissolved.

3 Simmer over low heat, stirring frequently, for 1 hour or until the butter thickens to resemble applesauce.

4 Spoon the butter into warmed sterilized jars, seal, and label.

Makes about 5 cups

CIDER-APPLE BUTTER

INGREDIENTS

2 lb eating apples

2 lb cooking apples

1$^1/_2$ cups cider

sugar

1 tsp ground coriander

1 Coarsely chop the apples, without peeling or coring them. Put the apples into a saucepan, add the cider, and bring to a boil. Simmer, stirring occasionally, for 25–30 minutes or until the apples are very soft. Press the apples through a plastic sieve set over a nonmetallic bowl.

2 Measure the pulp. For each $^1/_2$ cup pulp, measure 4$^1/_2$ Tb sugar. Warm the sugar (see box, page 44). Return the pulp to the pan, add the sugar and coriander, and stir over low heat until the sugar has completely dissolved.

3 Simmer over low heat, stirring frequently, for 30 minutes or until the butter thickens to resemble applesauce.

4 Spoon the butter into warmed sterilized jars, seal, and label.

Makes about 3 cups

VARIATION
Give a slightly tangier taste to this all-time favorite butter, by using Spiced Pickling Vinegar (see recipe, page 120) in place of the cider, and ground cinnamon instead of the coriander. Add the finely grated zest of 1 lemon with the spice.

DAMSON SPREAD

INGREDIENTS

6 lb damson plums

1¼ cups water

sugar, warmed
(see box, page 44)

1 Put the damsons and water into a preserving pan and bring to a boil. Simmer, stirring occasionally, for 30 minutes or until tender.

2 Press the damsons and juice through a plastic sieve set over a nonmetallic bowl. Discard the pits. Weigh the sieved pulp and return it to the pan with an equal weight of warmed sugar. Stir over low heat until the sugar has completely dissolved.

3 Bring to a boil and simmer, stirring, for 40–45 minutes. The pulp should be thick and firm enough that when a wooden spoon is drawn across the bottom of the pan, it will not move.

4 Spoon the spread into warmed sterilized jars, to within ⅛ inch of the tops. Seal and label.

Makes about 5½ cups

GUAVA SPREAD

INGREDIENTS

1 lb canned guavas

1 cup sugar, warmed
(see box, page 44)

2 Tb lemon juice

This spread is a quick, no-fuss preserve with lots of tropical flavor.

1 Strain the guavas and measure the juice. You will need 7 Tb guava juice from the can. Chop the guavas coarsely and put with the measured juice into a food processor. Purée the mixture until it is smooth.

2 Put the purée, warmed sugar, and lemon juice into a saucepan. Stir over low heat until the sugar has completely dissolved. Simmer over low heat for 12 minutes. The pulp should be thick and firm enough that when a wooden spoon is drawn across the bottom of the pan, it will not move.

3 Spoon the spread into warmed sterilized jars, to within ⅛ inch of the tops. Seal and label.

Makes about 1½ cups

DID YOU KNOW?
Guavas are an oval tropical fruit with yellow to green skin and an off-white to red flesh. This recipe is made with canned guavas so that no preparation is needed.

PLUM AND LEMON SPREAD

INGREDIENTS

6 lb plums

1¼ cups water

sugar, warmed
(see box, page 44)

finely grated zest and juice
of 2 lemons

1 Put the plums and water into a preserving pan and bring to a boil. Simmer, stirring occasionally, for 30 minutes.

2 Press the plums and juice through a plastic sieve set over a nonmetallic bowl. Discard the pits. Weigh the sieved pulp and return it to the pan with an equal weight of warmed sugar. Add the lemon juice and zest. Stir over low heat until the sugar has completely dissolved.

3 Bring to a boil, then simmer over low heat, stirring frequently, for 40–45 minutes. The pulp should be thick and firm enough that when a wooden spoon is drawn across the bottom of the pan, it will not move.

4 Spoon the spread into warmed sterilized jars, to within ⅛ inch of the tops. Seal and label.

Makes about 5½ cups

FRUIT CURDS

LEMON CURD TARTS with their sharp, fruity tart flavor, are what we think of when curds are mentioned today, unless of course our minds stray back to childhood and Little Miss Muffet, who ate curds and whey until she was disturbed by a spider. These curd recipes, unlike Miss Muffet's curds, are enriched with butter and eggs. Although lemon curd is an undisputed favorite, there are other, equally delicate and delicious, fruit curds to beguile our palates and to take as gifts to friends. Oranges, limes, and other fruits can be used, and there is plenty of room to experiment.

Curds have the paradoxical virtue of not being good keepers. They must be refrigerated, and should not be left to languish on the refrigerator shelf, but must be used within a month. In any case, these preserves are better eaten sooner than later because their flavor does fade and their fresh quality is lost the longer they are kept.

Curds can be spread on bread, toast, or on plain cake. They can also form the base of a dessert, or be spooned over ice-cream with colorful pieces of fruit. And what better way to spend a miserably wet Sunday afternoon in winter than making a batch of curd tarts, baked in pie pastry that melts in the mouth, that recreate Sundays of the past?

MAKING FRUIT CURDS

❧ Select fresh ingredients, particularly fresh eggs. Superfine sugar is the preferred sweetener, because curds are cooked very gently and the fine granules will dissolve more easily.
❧ Finely grate the zest of the chosen citrus fruits and squeeze out the juice. Strain and measure the juice. Pour it into a nonmetallic bowl set over a pan of gently simmering water (or use a double boiler), and add the grated zest, butter, and sugar. Stir the mixture over low heat, with a wooden spoon, until the butter has melted and the sugar has completely dissolved. Lightly beat the eggs and strain into the mixture. Continue simmering, stirring, until the mixture is thick enough to coat the back of the spoon. Do not allow the contents of the bowl to boil. Curds require long slow cooking, so do not rush the process by increasing the heat.
❧ When the mixture has thickened, immediately pour it into warmed sterilized jars (see page 11). Because of their limited shelf life, curds are best made in small quantities and put into 1 cup jars. Fill them right to the tops, because the curd will shrink and thicken as it cools.

How to seal and store
Use wax paper rounds and plastic wrap covers because they help prevent curds from going moldy. Place a wax paper round on the top of the curd, smooth over any air pockets, and leave to cool. Place a dampened plastic wrap cover over the top, and secure with a rubber band. Label and keep in the refrigerator. Use within 1 month.

What can go wrong and why
If a curd is runny, it has been insufficiently cooked. If it is curdled, it was cooked over too high a heat.

LIGHTLY COOKED EGGS Curds are cooked over a gentle heat and do not reach a high enough temperature to thoroughly cook the eggs. If you are worried about the slight risk of salmonella from lightly cooked eggs, it is best not to eat curds.

LEMON CURD

The tang of this spread comes from the lively lemon, and the thick, luscious smoothness from the careful blending of fresh eggs, creamy butter, and fine-grained sugar. Lemon curd will only keep for a month in the refrigerator, but it is so delicious that it is unlikely to last this long anyway. Serve it on toast, in pies, or as a filling for cakes.

INGREDIENTS

6–8 large juicy lemons

1 cup unsalted butter

2½ cups superfine sugar

5 eggs

Makes about 3 cups

WAXED LEMONS
If the lemons are waxed, scrub them first to remove the coating before grating the zest.

1 ▶ Grate the zest from the lemons on the finest side of the grater. Squeeze the juice and strain it into a large measuring cup. You will need 1¼ cups lemon juice.

2 ▼ Cut the butter into small pieces. Put the pieces of butter into a glass bowl, along with the sugar, lemon zest and juice, set over a pan of gently simmering water. The bottom of the bowl should not touch the water, nor should the water boil rapidly. Stir the mixture until the butter has melted and the sugar has completely dissolved.

3 ▼Lightly beat the eggs in a bowl, but do not whisk them. Strain the eggs through a fine sieve into the lemon mixture. Simmer over low heat, stirring constantly with a wooden spoon, until the mixture thickens slightly. This will take 20–25 minutes. Do not allow the mixture to boil or it will curdle.

4 ▲As soon as the mixture is thick enough to coat the back of the spoon, remove the bowl from the pan of water.

5 ▲Pour into warmed sterilized jars. Place a wax paper round, waxed-side down, on top. Smooth over to remove any air pockets. Leave to cool.

6 ▲Cover with dampened plastic wrap circles. Label and store in the refrigerator.

*M*ORE CURD FLAVORS

Oranges, limes, and grapefruit all make delicious curds. By adapting the Lemon Curd recipe you can create a sweeter or tangier preserve. For a touch of sophistication, add a splash or two of a flavored liqueur.

Orange Curd
This curd is delicious served with warm crêpes and whipped cream, particularly if you squeeze extra orange juice on top. Follow the Lemon Curd recipe, using the juice of 3 medium oranges and the juice of 1 lemon instead of the juice of 6–8 lemons. Combine the squeezed juices from the oranges and lemon to obtain a total of 1¹/₄ cups.

Above, *Lime Curd;* **right,** *Orange Curd*

Lime Curd
Use limes to make a tangier spread; the juice and tiny flecks of grated zest will turn the curd a subtle shade of green. Lime Curd makes an unusual filling for a cake or a tasty topping for ice cream. You will need more limes than lemons for this curd (about 10 juicy ones) to get the 1¹/₄ cups of juice required.

Pink Grapefruit and Lime Curd
◀ Use the finely grated zest of 2 pink grapefruit and 1 lime for this curd, and combine the juices to ensure you have the amount you need. If the curd is too runny, thicken it by sprinkling a little rice flour into the mixture, stirring it in well.

Tipsy Curd
Stir a few spoonfuls of a rich liqueur, such as hazelnut or orange into the finished curd. Tipsy curd is delicious when spread generously in a pastry pie shell, then piled high with sliced tropical fruit.

DID YOU KNOW?
Tangy fruit curds, simply spread on bread or between layers of sponge cake, were popular teatime treats in Victorian and Edwardian England. They were also used as a fragrant filling for trifles and piped into tartlets in elegant sweet swirls.

In her book *Modern Cookery for Private Families,* the nineteenth century cookbook writer Eliza Acton used a type of lemon curd as a filling for little puff pastry tarts. In addition to eggs, sugar, pounded butter, and lemon, she instructed the reader to "strew lightly in a spoonful of flour, well dried and sifted." Most modern fruit curds do not include flour, although the idea of adding a thickener is a good one if the curd seems a little runny – rice flour is suggested in Pink Grapefruit and Lime Curd for exactly this reason.

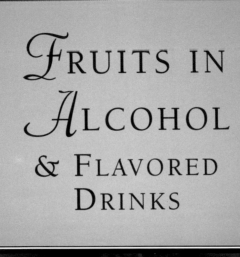

Fruits in Alcohol
& Flavored Drinks

FRUITS IN ALCOHOL

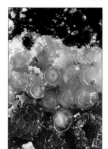

NOTHING IS QUITE so luxurious as fruit that has soaked up the perfumes of fortified wine, spirits, or liqueurs and, in turn, given its own flavor to the macerating liquid. Something quite astonishing happens to everyday pitted prunes when they have spent some time immersed in port.

Rum, gin, and brandy all have a strong affinity for summer and fall fruits, but almost any kind of alcohol can be used. Kirsch, for example, complements full-flavored fruits, such as raspberries, blackberries, loganberries, and pineapples; whiskey steeps well with grapes, and apricots take on a wonderful new flavor after being soaked in orange curaçao. Some cooked fruits can be preserved in wine, but they will last longer if used in combination with a spirit.

Fruits in alcohol, sweetened with sugar, look beautiful, taste even better, and are easy to make with only a little time and effort. They are superb when served as desserts, and their spiciness makes them great accompaniments to roast meats, game, and poultry, especially duck.

MAKING FRUITS IN ALCOHOL

❧ Choose your fruits; they must be just ripe. If they are overripe they will not retain their shape in the alcohol. Pick over the fruits, removing any moldy or bruised parts. Wash and dry the fruits and remove pits, if necessary. Remove and discard any excess peel, seeds, and cores from fruits such as pears. Soft fruits, such as berries, black currants, apricots, papayas, and peaches, can be used raw, while firmer ones, such as apples and hard plums, may require light cooking first.

❧ Pack the fruits in warmed sterilized jars (see page 11), either in layers with sugar or in a sugar syrup. Warm the jars if the ingredients used are hot. White sugar is the usual choice of sweetener, but light brown sugar can be used for flavor, or if a darker color is preferred. Shake the jars from time to time during the early days of storage, to help dissolve the sugar (unless a syrup is used) and blend it with the alcohol.

❧ Pour the chosen alcohol over the fruits to completely cover them, making sure there are no air pockets between them. The amount of liquid can vary, depending on the size of the fruits and the amount of sugar used, so make sure you have plenty of the chosen alcohol in stock.

❧ Spices, such as whole cloves, cinnamon sticks, and allspice berries can be added to the fruits in alcohol for extra flavor.

How to seal and store
Seal tightly, with noncorrosive screw-top lids. An airtight seal is required to prevent the alcohol from evaporating. Leave the fruits in a cool dark place for at least 1 month and preferably longer before using to allow the flavors to develop. Shake the jars occasionally to blend the sugar and flavorings. As long as the fruits are covered by the alcohol, they should keep for about 1 year, and the flavor will improve over this time.

What can go wrong and why
Some fruits have a tendency to float to the top of the liquid. Prevent this either by filling the jar with fruits to the very top or by placing a small coffee saucer in the top of the jar to hold the fruits down. Remove the saucer after about 1 week, after which time the fruits should remain in place. Make sure the fruits are covered with alcohol before sealing the jar. Refrigerate after opening. If the alcohol has evaporated, and left the fruits exposed, the jar has not been sealed tightly enough.

SUMMER FRUITS IN KIRSCH

A delicious way to preserve soft fruits, this recipe can be made either all at once, or throughout the summer as the different fruits ripen. If you layer the fruit over a period of time, keep it below the level of the alcohol by putting a lightly weighted saucer in the jar. When the last fruits have been layered, add kirsch to cover and reseal.

INGREDIENTS

1¹/₂ lb mixed summer fruits, e.g. raspberries, boysenberries, blueberries, small strawberries, blackberries, redcurrants, whitecurrants, and blackcurrants

1¹/₄ cups sugar

about 1¹/₄ cups kirsch

Makes about 1 quart

1 ◄Pick over the fruits, removing any leaves, moldy or damaged parts, hulls, and stalks. For the currants, run a fork along the stalks to remove the berries. Wash the fruits in a plastic sieve or colander and dry on paper towels.

2 ► Layer the fruits and sugar in a sterilized jar, to within 1 inch of the top of the jar.

TWICE THE FUN
Alcohol-drenched fruits make an intoxicating dessert, while the berry-flavored kirsch can be drunk separately

3 ▲Pour in the kirsch to cover the fruits by about ¹/₂ inch, making sure there are no air pockets left between the fruits. Seal the jar and label.

4 Keep in a cool dark place for 2–3 months before using to allow the flavors to develop, tipping the jar occasionally so the sugar dissolves.

Mangoes in Brandy

INGREDIENTS

3–4 large mangoes

1 cup sugar

1³/4 cups brandy

1 Cut each mango on both sides of the pit; slice the flesh away from the pit and discard the pit. Peel the mango slices and cut the flesh into even-sized chunks. There should be about 2 lb mango chunks.

2 Pack the mango cubes into sterilized jars, layering them with the sugar as you go. Leave 1 inch at the tops of the jars.

3 Pour in the brandy to cover the mango by ¹/2 inch, making sure there are no air pockets between the pieces of fruit. Seal the jars, label, and shake well.

4 Keep in a cool dark place for at least 2 months before using to allow the flavors to develop. Shake from time to time during the first week of storage to make sure all the sugar dissolves in the brandy.

Makes about 2 cups

Pears in Vodka

INGREDIENTS

2 lb ripe pears

2¹/4 cups sugar

2¹/3 cups vodka

1 Peel, quarter, and core the pears quickly to prevent discoloration. Pack the pears into sterilized jars, layering them with the sugar as you go. Leave 1 inch at the tops of the jars.

2 Pour in enough vodka to cover the pears by ¹/2 inch, making sure there are no air pockets between the pieces of fruit. Seal the jars, label, and shake well.

3 Keep in a cool dark place for at least 2–3 months before using to allow the flavors to develop. Shake from time to time during the first week of storage to make sure all the sugar dissolves in the vodka.

Makes about 3 cups

Plums in Rum

INGREDIENTS

3 lb plums

1 cup sugar

7 Tb water

1¹/3 cups golden or white rum

1 Prick the plums all over with a sterilized needle or a wooden toothpick. In a saucepan, combine the sugar and water and simmer over low heat, stirring with a wooden spoon, until the sugar has completely dissolved. Add the plums and simmer for 5 minutes. Remove the pan from the heat and allow to cool.

2 Pack the plums and syrup into sterilized jars, then slowly pour in the rum to cover them by 1 inch. Seal the jars, label, and shake well.

3 Keep in a cool dark place for at least 1 month before using to allow the flavors to develop. Check after the first day or so to be sure the plums are still covered by the liquid. Add more rum, if necessary and reseal.

Makes about 2 cups

RUMTOPF Use a mixture of fruits, such as cherries, strawberries, apricots, nectarines, and plums, to make a traditional *Rumtopf*. This German preserve is made in stages as the fruits become available, to keep until Advent. Layer each addition of fruit with sugar and cover with rum as directed.

PRUNES IN PORT

INGREDIENTS

1 lb pitted prunes

1³/₄–2¹/₄ cups tawny port

Serve the prunes with roast pork or game or as a simple dessert with ice cream, spooning the port over it. Or drink the port as a liqueur.

1 Pack the prunes into a sterilized jar and pour in about 1³/₄ cups port to cover the prunes by 1¹/₂ inches. Cover and reserve the remaining port.

2 Seal the jar and label. Keep the prunes in a cool dark place.

3 Check the prunes in a day or two. Once they have soaked up so much port that they are no longer covered, pour in the remaining port to cover. Reseal and leave for 1 month before using to allow the flavors to develop.

Makes about 1 quart

TIPSY APRICOTS

INGREDIENTS

1¹/₂–2 lb apricots

1²/₃ cups sugar

1–1¹/₄ cups orange curaçao

1–1¹/₄ cups dark rum

1 Prick the apricots all over with a sterilized needle or a wooden toothpick.

2 Pack the apricots into sterilized jars, layering them with the sugar as you go. Leave at least 1 inch at the tops of the jars.

3 Mix the orange curaçao with the rum in a glass measuring cup. Slowly pour the mixed alcohols into the jars to cover the apricots by ¹/₂ inch, making sure there are no air pockets left between the fruits.

4 Seal the jars and label. Shake the jars so that the sugar can start to blend and dissolve into the alcohol.

5 Keep in a cool dark place for at least 2 months before using to allow the flavors to develop. Shake from time to time during the first week to of storage to make sure all the sugar dissolves in the curaçao and rum.

Makes about 3 cups

VARIATION
Mandarins or clementines can be preserved in the same syrup as apricots. Peel the fruits, keeping them whole (there is no need to prick them.) Pack into jars, layering with the sugar and the grated zest of 2 oranges. Continue as directed in step 3.

PEARS IN BRANDY

INGREDIENTS

3 lb firm ripe pears

¹/₂ cup superfine sugar

2 cups brandy

1 Peel, quarter, and core the pears. If the fruits are small, just halve and core them.

2 Put the pear quarters and the sugar into a saucepan with just enough water to cover. Cover the pan and simmer for 30 minutes, until the pears are tender and the sugar has completely dissolved. Allow the pears to cool, then transfer to sterilized jars, using a slotted spoon.

3 Boil the pear juice over high heat until it has thickened and reduced to a scant cup. Pour it over the pears. Pour in the brandy, to within 1 inch of the tops.

4 Seal the jars and label. Keep in a cool dark place for at least 1 month before using to allow the flavors to develop.

Makes about 3³/₄ cups

COOK'S TIP To prevent discoloration, cover the peeled pears with lemon juice, or place in acidulated salted water made with 1 tsp salt and 1 tsp citric acid to each 1 quart water.

GRAPES IN WHISKEY

INGREDIENTS

2–2$^{1}/_{4}$ lb seedless grapes

2 cups sugar

2$^{1}/_{2}$–3 cups whiskey

1 Prick the grapes all over with a sterilized needle or a wooden toothpick. Pack the grapes into sterilized jars, layering them with the sugar as you go. Leave about 1 inch space at the tops of the jars.

2 Slowly pour in the whiskey to cover the grapes by $^{1}/_{2}$ inch, making sure there are no air pockets.

3 Seal the jars, label, and shake well. Keep in a cool dark place for at least 2–3 months before using to allow the flavors to develop. Shake from time to time during the first week of storage to make sure that all the sugar dissolves.

Makes about 6 cups

PEARS IN RED WINE

INGREDIENTS

2$^{1}/_{3}$ cups red wine

2$^{1}/_{4}$ cups sugar

4$^{1}/_{2}$ lb pears

2 cinnamon sticks

brandy

VARIATION The pears can be replaced by mixed soft red fruits, such as strawberries, raspberries, and red currants. Pack, uncooked, into sterilized jars as directed in step 1. Prepare the red wine syrup as directed, adding 6 crushed cardamom pods. Strain the syrup and pour over the red fruits to cover.

1 Put the red wine and sugar into a preserving pan and stir over low heat until the sugar has completely dissolved.

2 Peel, quarter, and core the pears, and add to the pan with the cinnamon sticks. Bring the mixture to a boil, lower the heat, and simmer the pears for 5–10 minutes or until they are just tender. Take care not to overcook. Discard the cinnamon sticks. With a slotted spoon, transfer the pears to sterilized jars, to within 1 inch of the tops of the jars.

3 Increase the heat and boil the syrup rapidly, without stirring, for 5 minutes. Strain the syrup into a glass measuring cup and make up to 3 cups with brandy. Pour the syrup and brandy mixture into the jars to cover the pears by $^{1}/_{2}$ inch. Seal the jars and label. Keep in a cool dark place for at least 2 months before using to allow the flavors to develop.

Makes about 6 cups

PAPAYAS IN RUM

INGREDIENTS

3 papayas

$^{1}/_{2}$ cup raw pistachios

1 cup sugar

1 cup plus 5 Tb rum

1 Peel and halve the papayas. Scoop out the seeds. Cut the flesh into large cubes. There should be about 1$^{1}/_{4}$ lb fruit.

2 Put the pistachios into a bowl and pour over boiling water to cover. Leave for 1 minute, then drain and transfer to a bowl of cold water. Drain again, then rub off the skins with your fingers.

3 Pack the papayas and pistachios into sterilized jars, layering them with the sugar as you go. Leave about 1 inch at the tops of the jars. Pour in the rum to cover the fruits and nuts by $^{1}/_{2}$ inch, making sure there are no air pockets.

4 Seal the jars, label, and shake well. Keep in a cool dark place for at least 2–3 months before using to allow the flavors to develop. Shake from time to time during the first week of storage to make sure that all the sugar dissolves.

Makes about 4 cups

PINEAPPLES IN KIRSCH

INGREDIENTS

2 ripe pineapples, total weight about 4¹/₂ lb with leaves

2 cups sugar

1¹/₂–2 cups kirsch

Kirsch is a cherry brandy which has a natural affinity with pineapple.

1 Slice the tops off the pineapples. Cut the peel off in strips, cutting deep enough to remove the "eyes" with the peel. Cut the pineapples across into thick slices and cut out and discard the hard central core from each slice. Dice the flesh.

2 Pack the pineapple into sterilized jars, layering it with the sugar as you go. Leave about 1 inch space at the tops of the jars.

3 Pour in the kirsch to cover the pineapple by ¹/₂ inch, making sure there are no air pockets between the chunks of fruits. Seal the jars, label, and shake well.

4 Keep in a cool dark place for at least 1–2 months before using to allow the flavors to develop. Shake from time to time during the first week of storage to make sure all the sugar dissolves.

Makes about 4 cups

RAISINS IN GENEVER WITH JUNIPER BERRIES

INGREDIENTS

1¹/₂ lb seedless raisins

2 cups sugar

1 Tb juniper berries

3–4 cups genever gin

Gin is a spirit that is made from distilling juniper berries. It is therefore appropriate for gin and juniper to be mixed together in this recipe.

1 Layer the raisins with the sugar in sterilized jars, adding a few juniper berries with each layer.

2 Pour in the genever gin to cover the raisins, continuing to the tops of the jars and making sure that there are no air pockets between the raisins. Seal the jars, label, and shake well.

3 The next day, check to see that the raisins have not risen above the level of the alcohol. If they have, remove a layer, and re-seal. Keep in a cool dark place for at least 2 months before using to allow the flavors to develop. Shake from time to time during the first week of storage to make sure all the sugar dissolves.

Makes about 6 cups

DID YOU KNOW?
Genever is a type of Dutch gin with a strong flavor. In Holland, raisins in genever are traditionally served in glasses on New Year's Eve. If you cannot get genever, ordinary gin can be used.

BRANDIED PEACHES

INGREDIENTS

1¹/₂–2 lb peaches

2 cups sugar

1¹/₂–2 cups brandy

1 Halve and pit the peaches. The fruits can also be peeled for a classic effect, but this is not necessary.

2 Pack the peach halves into sterilized jars, layering with the sugar as you go. Leave at least 1 inch at the tops of the jars.

3 Pour in the brandy to cover the peaches by ¹/₂ inch, making sure there are no air pockets between the fruits. Seal the jars, label, and shake well.

4 Keep in a cool dark place for at least 2–3 months before using to allow the flavors to develop. Shake from time to time during the first week of storage to make sure all the sugar dissolves.

Makes about 2 quarts

FLAVORED WINES & SPIRITS

ALMOST ALL commercially flavored wines and spirits are made according to jealously guarded formulas. Aquavit with caraway seeds, gin with juniper berries, sambuca and ouzo with aniseed, are some of the best known. Fruit brandies, known as *alcools blancs,* are commercially distilled from fresh fruits, the most popular being plums, pears, black cherries, and raspberries, while the production of vermouths requires a complicated process involving herbs, sugar syrup, alcohol, and all kinds of equipment.

Yet flavoring wines and spirits is not altogether out of reach of the home cook. Vanilla and cherry brandies are easy to make, while red-hot chilies can transform the taste of sherry. Dry white wine is delicious when delicately flavored with fruit, with the aid of a little sugar syrup. All it requires is enough patience to wait while the fruits and wine exchange flavors. Although the wine will be the winner, the strained-out fruits can often be used, perhaps as an ingredient in a homemade ice-cream or sorbet.

MAKING FLAVORED WINES & SPIRITS

❧ Sterilize a large glass jar (see page 11) in which to steep the flavorings and alcohol.

❧ Choose the ingredients. Fresh berries and fruits with pits are the best choices of fruits. Herbs and spices and other seasonings should be as fresh as possible. If flavoring with spice, use whole spices. The choice of alcohol depends on personal preference – any kind can be used, provided that it has an alcoholic content of at least 37.5% by volume.

❧ If fruits are being used as a flavoring, wash and dry them first. Remove any stalks, and any moldy or bruised parts. Halve and pit fruits such as apricots. Cherries do not require pitting, but should be pricked all over with a sterilized needle or a wooden toothpick so that their flavor and color can be released into the alcohol.

❧ Put the fruits into the prepared jar, layering them with sugar or covering with a sugar syrup, then add the alcohol. For herb- and spice-infused wines and spirits, simply insert the flavorings into sterilized bottles (lightly bruising fresh herbs first), and pour in the chosen alcohol.

❧ Allow the flavors to develop before using, shaking the jar from time to time. Allow about 3 months for fruit-infused spirits. Wines should be left to steep for 2–3 days if combined with fresh ingredients, and for up to 4 weeks if dried flavorings, such as apricots, herbs, and spices, are used.

❧ Strain the flavored wine or spirit through a double layer of cheesecloth into sterilized bottles.

How to seal and store
Seal the bottles tightly with noncorrosive screw-top lids or corks. Choose new corks and secure them into the bottles with a wooden mallet. Spirits keep well and last almost indefinitely when stored in a cool dark place. Flavored wines do not last as long. Once opened, the flavor will deteriorate after a few days unless the wine has been mixed with other preservatives (sugar and spirits).

What can go wrong and why
If ground spices are used for flavoring, the wine or spirit will turn cloudy. Always use whole spices. If the drink lacks flavor, the infusing time has been too short, or the ingredients are too bland.

CHERRY BRANDY

Traditionally, Morello cherries are used for this classic fruited spirit because they are less sweet than other varieties, but you can use any dark, flavorful cherry instead. Let the brandy mature before decanting it into bottles, in time to give as a cheering winter gift. And don't neglect the cherries. After being strained, they are delicious topped with freshly whipped cream.

INGREDIENTS

1 lb cherries

scant $^1/2$ cup sugar

2 drops of almond extract

$2^1/3$ cups brandy

Makes about 1 quart

1 ◄ Remove all the cherry stalks. Prick each cherry all over with a sterilized needle or a wooden toothpick.

2 ◄ Layer the cherries with the sugar in a large sterilized jar, to within 1 inch of the top. Add the almond extract to the jar.

3 ▶ Pour in the brandy to cover the cherries by $^1/2$ inch. Seal the jar and shake well. Keep in a cool dark place for at least 3 months before using to allow the flavors to develop. Shake the jar from time to time.

4 ▶ Line a funnel with a double layer of cheesecloth and strain the brandy through it into a sterilized bottle. Seal the bottle and label. The brandy is now ready to use.

BURGUNDY BRANDY
The brandy has taken on a deep rich color from the cherries.

Sloe Gin

INGREDIENTS

1 lb sloes

1 cups sugar

4 cups gin

a few drops of almond extract (optional)

Sloes grow wild in the U.S., and are related to the plum.

1 Remove any stalks from the sloes. Prick each sloe all over with a sterilized needle or a wooden toothpick. Layer the sloes and sugar into a sterilized jar. Pour in the gin to cover the sloes completely, and add the almond extract, if using. Seal the jar and shake well. Keep in a cool dark place for about 3 months before using to allow the flavors to develop. Shake the jar occasionally.

2 Line a funnel with a double layer of cheesecloth and strain the flavored gin through it into sterilized bottles. Seal the bottles and label. The gin is now ready to use.

Makes about 5 1/2 cups

Apricot Wine with Brandy

INGREDIENTS

1/2 cup dried apricots

1/3 cup sugar

1 bottle of dry white wine

2 Tb brandy

1 Coarsely chop the apricots and put them into a saucepan with the sugar. Pour in just enough water to cover. Cover the pan and leave to stand for 2 hours. Simmer the apricots, stirring occasionally, for 10 minutes or until the fruit is soft and tender.

2 Put the apricots and their syrup into a sterilized jar and slowly pour in the white wine and brandy to cover. Seal the jar and shake well. Keep in a cool dark place for 3 weeks before using to allow the flavors to develop. Shake the jar occasionally.

3 Line a funnel with a double layer of cheesecloth and strain the flavored wine through it into sterilized bottles. Seal the bottles and label. The wine is now ready to use.

Makes about 3 2/3 cups

COOK'S TIP Serve Apricot Wine with Brandy well chilled, as an aperitif. For a special occasion, pour it into a punch bowl and float nasturtium flowers on top. The strained apricots can be served separately as a dessert, or as an accompaniment to savory game, meat, or poultry dishes.

Blushing Strawberry Wine

INGREDIENTS

1/2 lb strawberries

3 sprigs of fresh lemon balm

1 sprig of fresh rosemary

1 sprig of fresh hyssop

1 bottle of semi-sweet rosé wine

This is a refreshing early summer drink which can be served either undiluted or in tall glasses with a splash of sparkling water. Float vivid blue borage flowers or a sprig of lemon balm in each glass, for an attractive finish.

1 Hull and slice the strawberries. Lightly bruise the herbs to release their flavor. Put the strawberries and herbs in a sterilized jar and pour in the wine to cover

2 Seal the jar and shake well. Keep in a cool dark place for 2 days before using to allow the flavors to develop. Shake the jar occasionally.

3 Line a funnel with a double layer of cheesecloth and strain the flavored wine through it into sterilized bottles. Seal the bottles, label, and keep in the refrigerator. The wine is now ready to use.

Makes about 3 2/3 cups

Whiskey Liqueur with Herbs

INGREDIENTS

3/4 cup clear honey

3²/₃ cups whiskey

2 sprigs of dried fennel

2 sprigs of dried thyme

4 whole cloves

2 cinnamon sticks

1 Put the honey into a saucepan and heat just until warm. Remove from the heat and gradually stir in the whiskey until the honey has completely dissolved. Transfer to a sterilized jar and add the herbs and spices. Seal the jar and shake well. Keep in a cool dark place for at least 4 months before using to allow the flavors to develop. Shake the jar occasionally.

2 Line a funnel with a double layer of cheesecloth and strain the flavored whiskey through it into sterilized bottles. Seal the bottles and label. The whiskey is now ready to use.

Makes about 1 quart

Cassis

INGREDIENTS

2 cups blackcurrants

2¹/₃ cups dry white wine

about 3 cups sugar

about 1 cup brandy or gin

VARIATIONS Cassis is most commonly made with brandy or gin, but vodka can be used instead. A small cinnamon stick and a whole clove can be added to the syrup to give a touch of spice.

1 Lightly crush the blackcurrants in a large glass bowl. Stir in the wine, cover, and leave in a cool dark place for 2 days.

2 Blend the blackcurrant mixture in a food processor or blender. Line a large funnel with a double layer of cheesecloth and strain the liquid through it. Measure the strained liquid. For each 1¹/₄ cups liquid, measure 1 cup sugar. Put the liquid and sugar into a saucepan and stir over low heat until the sugar has completely dissolved. Do not boil. Simmer over low heat, stirring, for 45 minutes.

3 Cool, then measure. For 3 parts blackcurrant liquid, add 1 part brandy or gin. Pour into sterilized bottles. Seal the bottles and label. Keep in a cool dark place for 2–3 days before using to allow the flavors to develop.

Makes about 6 cups

Hot Pepper Sherry or Rum

INGREDIENTS

6 hot red chilies, fresh or dried

2 cups dry sherry or light rum

This is a potent brew, so add a few drops sparingly to stews or sauces.

1 Put the chilies into a sterilized bottle with the sherry or rum. Seal, label, and shake well. Keep in a cool dark place for 2 weeks before using to allow the flavors to develop. Shake the bottle occasionally. Remove the chilies before using.

Makes about 2 cups

Vanilla Brandy

INGREDIENTS

2 whole vanilla beans

2 cups brandy

STRAWBERRY SURPRISE
Blushing Strawberry Wine is glamorized with flower garnish.

1 Cut the vanilla beans lengthwise to release their flavor. Put them into a sterilized bottle with the brandy. Seal, label, and shake well. Keep in a cool dark place for 3 weeks before using to allow the flavors to develop. Shake the bottle occasionally.

2 Remove the vanilla beans. The brandy is now ready to use.

Makes about 2 cups

Fruit Cordials & Syrups

QUENCH A SUMMER THIRST with a nonalcoholic fruit cordial or syrup diluted with soda, water, even lemonade. A syrup or cordial is often the base for an alcohol punch or cocktail. A single fruit can be used for a syrup, but any fruits can be combined in a recipe as long as some of them are sour enough to balance the sweetness of the sugar. Too sweet a taste would lack the refreshing tartness that makes cordials such ideal companions for hot sunny days. However, these drinks are welcome at any time, thirst knows no season.

The fruit cordials and syrups are concentrated, and a little goes a long way, so they are very economical, especially if you are able to pick your own wild fruits for free. The best fruits are juicy berries, such as strawberries, raspberries, loganberries, and blackberries. Citrus fruits are good too: use both zest and pulp to maximize the citrus flavor. Even exotic tropical fruits are ideal ingredients for cordials and syrups, with kiwifruit, passion fruit, kumquats, and pineapples giving a subtly fragrant flavor.

Making Fruit Cordials & Syrups

❦ Choose the fruits. Fully ripe or even slightly overripe fruits with plenty of flavor are best for cordials or syrups. Underripe fruits lack both flavor and juice. White sugar is the usual choice of sweetener. Make sure you have enough sugar, because the exact amount is often calculated after the juice has been extracted from the fruits.

❦ Prepare the fruits; discard any moldy or bruised parts, and wash and dry the fruits, as necessary. Then extract the juice. This is done by lightly heating, pressing, or squeezing the fruits. The aim is to do this without destroying the flavor of the fruits, so do not overcook them.

❦ Strain the purée through a double layer of cheesecloth, then lightly squeeze it to extract as much juice as possible.

❦ Add sugar to the juice and dissolve over very low heat. The mixture is then boiled for about 5 minutes.

❦ Leave the mixture to cool, then pour into sterilized bottles (see page 11), to within ¹⁄₈ inch of the tops.

How to seal and store

Seal tightly with screw-top lids or plastic stoppers. Corks can also be used (see Flavored Vinegars, page 117). The recipes in this section do not include any special heat treatments nor do they contain sufficient sugar to allow for long storage, so the cordials and syrups should be drunk straightaway, or kept in the refrigerator for only 3–4 weeks. Alternatively, they can be frozen. A convenient way to freeze them is in ice cube trays: pour in the fruit drink, leaving room for it to expand. When frozen, turn the cubes out into plastic bags and keep in the freezer. One ice cube will be enough for a 1 cup drink, ideal for making in a hurry.

What can go wrong and why

If a cordial or syrup develops a sediment at the bottom of the bottle it is merely tiny pieces of pulp that have slipped through during straining. Simply pour the cordial or syrup with care so that the sediment is not disturbed.

PINEAPPLE AND LIME SYRUP

This syrup has a taste of the tropics, making it a wonderful base for rum punches and daiquiris. Alternatively, dilute it with a little sparkling water and serve as a cooling nonalcoholic drink. Lots of ice cubes and fresh twists of citrus zest will give it added zip.

INGREDIENTS

2 pineapples, total weight about 4¹/₂ lb

1¹/₄ cups water

about ³/₄ cup sugar

juice of 3 limes

Makes about 2¹/₂ cups

1 ▸ Slice the tops off the pineapples. Cut off the peel in strips, cutting deep enough to remove the "eyes." Slice the pineapples and cut out and discard the hard central core from each slice; finely chop the flesh.

2 ▾ Put the pineapple into a saucepan with the water and bring to a boil. Simmer over low heat for 20 minutes or until the fruit is soft and pulpy. Mash with a potato masher.

3 ▾ Line a plastic sieve with a double layer of cheesecloth. Strain the pulp through it into a bowl. Gather the corners of the cheesecloth together and squeeze to extract all the juice possible. Discard the pulp. Measure the juice. For each 1¹/₄ cups juice, measure ¹/₂ cup sugar.

ZESTY FINISH
Juicy limes add a refreshing tang to pineapple syrup.

4 ▸ Pour the juice back into the saucepan, add the sugar, and stir over low heat until the sugar has completely dissolved. Stir in the lime juice.

5 Bring the mixture to a boil and simmer over low heat for 5 minutes. Cool for 5 minutes, then pour into sterilized bottles, to within ¹/₈ inch of the tops. Seal the bottles, label, and keep in the refrigerator. The syrup is now ready to use.

STRAWBERRY SYRUP

INGREDIENTS

3 quarts
strawberries, hulled

sugar

juice of 2 lemons

1 Purée the strawberries in a food processor or blender. Line a plastic sieve with a double layer of cheesecloth. Strain the pulp through it into a nonmetallic bowl. Gather the corners of the cheesecloth and lightly squeeze to extract all the juice possible. Discard the pulp.

2 Measure the juice. For each $2^1/_3$ cups juice, measure $1^1/_2$ cups sugar. Pour the juice into a saucepan, add the sugar, and stir over low heat until the sugar has completely dissolved. Stir in the lemon juice. Cool for 5 minutes.

3 Pour into sterilized bottles, to within $^1/_8$ inch of the tops. Seal the bottles, label, and keep in the refrigerator.

Makes about 1 quart

VARIATIONS

Other strongly acidic fruits, such as raspberries, can be used to make this syrup. Blackcurrants can also be used, in which case add $3^1/_2$ cups water while the syrup is cooling.

LOGANBERRY AND LEMON BALM CORDIAL

INGREDIENTS

4 lb loganberries

4 sprigs of lemon balm

$2^1/_3$ cups water

sugar

juice of 2 lemons

1 Put the loganberries and the lemon balm into a saucepan with the water, and bring to a boil. Simmer for 8–10 minutes or until the fruit is soft. Mash with a potato masher.

2 Line a plastic sieve with a double layer of cheesecloth. Strain the pulp through it into a nonmetallic bowl. Gather the corners of the cheesecloth and lightly squeeze to extract all the juice possible.

3 Measure the juice. For each $2^1/_3$ cups juice, measure $1^1/_8$ cups sugar. Pour the juice back into the saucepan, add the sugar, and stir over low heat until the sugar has completely dissolved. Stir in the lemon juice. Bring the mixture to a boil and simmer for 5 minutes. Cool for 5 minutes.

4 Pour into sterilized bottles, to within $^1/_8$ inch of the tops. Seal the bottles, label, and keep in the refrigerator.

Makes about 1 quart

KUMQUAT CORDIAL

INGREDIENTS

1 lb kumquats

$1^1/_4$ cups water

juice of 10 oranges, about 3 cups

sugar

1 Slice the kumquats and put the fruit slices into a saucepan with the water. Bring to a boil and simmer for 30 minutes or until the fruit is very soft.

2 Line a plastic sieve with a double layer of cheesecloth. Strain the pulp through it into a nonmetallic bowl. Gather the corners of the cheesecloth and squeeze to extract all the juice possible.

3 Mix the kumquat juice with the orange juice. Measure the total amount of juice. For each $2^1/_3$ cups juice, measure $1^1/_8$ cups sugar. Pour the juice back into the saucepan, add the sugar, and stir over low heat until the sugar has completely dissolved. Cool for 5 minutes.

4 Pour into sterilized bottles, to within $^1/_8$ inch of the tops. Seal the bottles, label, and keep in the refrigerator.

Makes about 1 quart

St. Clement's Cordial

INGREDIENTS

juice of 8 oranges, about
3 cups

juice of 6 lemons, about
1$^1/_3$ cups

finely grated zest of 2 oranges
and 2 lemons

4$^1/_2$ cups sugar

The name of this cordial was inspired by an English nursery rhyme.

1 Put the fruit juices and grated zest into a saucepan. Add the sugar and stir over low heat until the sugar has completely dissolved. Increase the heat and bring to just below the boiling point. Immediately remove from the heat. Leave to cool completely.

2 Line a plastic sieve with a double layer of cheesecloth. Strain the pulp through it into a nonmetallic bowl. Gather the corners of the cheesecloth and lightly squeeze to extract all the juice possible. Pour into sterilized bottles, to within $^1/_8$ inch of the tops. Seal the bottles, label and keep in the refrigerator.

Makes about 5$^1/_2$ cups

Blackberry and Apple Cordial

INGREDIENTS

4 lb blackberries

2$^1/_3$ cups apple juice

sugar

juice of 2 lemons

1 Put the blackberries into a large saucepan with the apple juice. Bring to a boil and simmer over very low heat for 20 minutes or until the fruit is soft. Mash with a potato masher. Line a plastic sieve with a double layer of cheesecloth. Strain the juice through it into a nonmetallic bowl. Gather the corners of the cheesecloth and lightly squeeze to extract all the juice possible.

2 Measure the juice. For each 2$^1/_3$ cups juice, measure 1 cup sugar. Pour the juice back into the saucepan, add the sugar, and stir over low heat until the sugar has completely dissolved. Stir in the lemon juice. Bring the mixture to a boil and simmer for 5 minutes. Cool for 5 minutes.

3 Pour into sterilized bottles, to within $^1/_8$ inch of the tops. Seal the bottles, label, and keep in the refrigerator.

Makes about 1 quart

Kiwi-Passion Fruit Syrup

INGREDIENTS

2 lb kiwifruit

about 8 passion fruit

sugar

These fragrant tropical fruits are delicious when combined together.

1 Peel and coarsely chop the kiwifruit. Halve the passion fruit and scoop out the seeds and flesh and discard the skins. Purée the flesh of both fruits in a food processor or blender.

2 Line a plastic sieve with a double layer of cheesecloth. Strain the pulp through it into a nonmetallic bowl. Gather the corners of the cheesecloth and squeeze to extract all the juice possible.

3 Measure the juice. For each $^2/_3$ cup juice, measure 1 cup sugar. Pour the juice into a saucepan, add the sugar, and stir over low heat until the sugar has completely dissolved. Bring the mixture to a boil and simmer for 5 minutes. Cool for 5 minutes.

4 Pour into sterilized bottles, to within $^1/_8$ inch of the tops. Seal the bottles, label, and keep in the refrigerator.

Makes about 2 cups

PASSION FRUIT
Use a small teaspoon to extract the yellow pulp and crunchy black seeds of the passion fruit.

Pickles, Chutneys, Relishes & Mustards

VEGETABLE & FRUIT PICKLES

PICKLING IS the perfect answer to nature's exhuberant harvest. Fruits and vegetables can be "put up" in jars and bottles to give a fillip to foods, adding a sharp and spicy accent to ordinary winter fare. The jewellike colors of ruby beets, emerald green beans, and moonstone shaped garlic cloves make attractive pickles. Fruit pickles can be made from hard or fleshy fruits like apples, peaches, and pears. Probably the most famous vegetable pickles are cucumber or dill pickles and pickled onions, though everything from asparagus to zucchini can take on a brine. Pickles might turn up with cocktails, but for most Americans a sandwich isn't lunch unless a pickle – tart or sweet, salty or piquant – accompanies it.

Pickles play an important part in many other cuisines, particularly those of the Middle and Far East. To the pickle-loving Japanese, any meal without pickles is simply incomplete. A favorite of theirs is pickled ginger, which takes a little time to prepare but is infinitely useful as a garnish. Other parts of the world have their own favorite foods for pickling. Oranges, dates, or cherries make exceedingly luxurious pickles, and spiced cranberries enchant with their exquisite pink color as well as their tart flavor. Green tomato pickles, pickled sweet red peppers, zucchini flavored with seeds and spices, or carrots scented with thyme and coriander and sweetened with sugar – the combination of foods for pickling seems almost endless.

MAKING VEGETABLE & FRUIT PICKLES

❧ Select the ingredients. Vinegar, added to prevent spoilage by microorganisms, is the main ingredient for preserving pickles. Use only good-quality bottled vinegar. Distilled white vinegar is the most economical vinegar for pickling and it does not impose its own character on the pickle. Malt vinegar is dark and potent but it is useful for making many pickles. Cider and wine vinegar may be recommended where the spicing is more delicate. Spiced Pickling Vinegar (see recipe, page 120) gives a good flavor to pickles. For a more sophisticated taste, vinegars flavored with herbs or fruits can be used (see Flavored Vinegar, pages 117–121). The general rule when choosing vinegar, is to match the vinegar to suit the type of vegetable or fruit you are pickling and to consider the overall color and flavor you want to create.

❧ Salt which may be used for salting vegetables before pickling is another essential preservative for many pickles. Choose sea salt or kosher salt, never table salt which contains chemical additives to keep it flowing freely. Sometimes the vinegar is sweetened; granulated sugar is the usual choice of sweetener, but brown sugar may be used for its flavor in certain spiced pickles. Many pickling recipes call for spices: use whole spices because they are easily removed and will also give a clear pickling liquid. Ground spices will cloud the vinegar.

❧ There is no real restriction on the type of vegetables that can be used in pickles, as long as they are firm, uniformly sized, young, and fresh. Avoid any vegetables that are obviously damaged or showing signs of dampness. Do not use any vegetables that are beginning to sprout green shoots. If pickling whole items, choose small sizes for easier packing. The most popular pickles are made with beets, onions, red and white cabbages, cauliflower, cucumbers, or a mixture of different vegetables. Mushrooms, artichokes, and bell peppers also make excellent pickles. Choose fruits that are not overripe and are as fresh as possible. Fruits such as melons, peaches, pears, and plums are usually pickled in sweetened vinegar, whereas lemons can be pickled in salt.

❧ Prepare the vegetables or fruits. Using a stainless steel knife, peel and trim the vegetables or fruits as appropriate. Remove any moldy or bruised parts. If cooking is required, steam the vegetables or cook the fruits in a light syrup.

❧ Some raw vegetables need to be salted or brined before they are pickled. This is to extract the moisture they contain so the vinegar can penetrate the food and preserve it. (Cooked fruits and vegetables do not need to be brined because the cooking process boils off any excess water.) The recipe may stipulate drybrining or wetbrining. For drybrining, the vegetables are layered with salt in a large nonmetallic bowl, left to stand overnight, and stirred occasionally during this time. For wetbrining, a solution of salt and water is poured over the vegetables, which are again left to stand overnight, and stirred occasionally. After brining, the vegetables must be drained, washed, and drained again to remove all the salt, then patted thoroughly dry with paper towels. Avoid using any metal utensils when brining.

❧ Pack the brined or cooked fruits or vegetables into dry sterilized jars (see page 11). Do not pack too tightly, because you need to leave space for the vinegar to surround them. Instead of packing single vegetables separately, layering different vegetables in the jar can create a decorative effect. Cooked vegetables can be left to stand for an hour in the jars so that any liquid that collects at the bottom can be drained off before proceeding.

❧ Cover the vegetables with vinegar, tapping the jars to prevent air pockets from forming. Fruits are pickled in hot syrup or vinegar or a mixture of both. Leave at least 1/2 inch space at the top of the jar after packing the fruits or vegetables. The vinegar can then be poured almost to the tops of the jars – ensuring the fruits or vegetables are well covered, even if some of the vinegar evaporates during storage.

How to seal and store

Seal the pickles tightly with noncorrosive screw-top lids. Pickles should be stored in a cool dark place, such as a pantry that is dry and well ventilated. Vegetable pickles are usually ready to eat after 2–3 weeks, but spiced pickled fruits should be left for about 2 months before using to allow the flavors to develop. As the pickles tend to absorb the vinegar during storage, it may be necessary to top up the jars with more vinegar after a day or two, to make sure the vegetables are always covered. Pickled vegetables and fruits that are covered with pure vinegar will last longer than those which are covered with a combination of water or oil and vinegar.

What can go wrong and why

Yellow spots sometimes appear on pickled onions. This is due to the formation of a harmless substance, and the onions can still be eaten. Certain vegetables, such as zucchini, will have a bitter taste if they are not brined or salted before they are pickled. If pickles do not keep well, it could be because they were not brined for long enough, so that too much moisture came out of them and diluted the vinegar. Alternatively, the vinegar may not have been up to strength and contained less than 5% acetic acid. Avoid boiling any vinegar solution for a long time because the acetic acid will lose its ability to keep stored pickles safe. Too short a salting or brining time can make the vinegar turn cloudy. If the pickles become soft, they may have been left too long before being eaten.

Air pockets will be trapped in the jars if the vegetables or fruits are packed too tightly, and the vinegar has not been able to completely cover them. Tapping the jars once they are filled will help remove any pockets that do form. Pickles will turn moldy on top if they are not covered with vinegar when being bottled. If the jars are not sealed correctly, the vinegar will evaporate, causing the contents of the jars to shrink and dry out. If lids are not noncorrosive, rust will form and contaminate the pickles.

> **DID YOU KNOW?** The idea of pickling vegetables and fruits is not a new one. In fact it is one of the most ancient forms of preserving foods, dating back to Greek and Roman times. The Romans had the advantage of having an extensive variety of foods to pickle, which they imported from the lands they conquered in Europe. Onions, lemons, plums, and peaches, as well as herbs, roots, and flowers, would all probably have fallen prey to the large pickling vases used as storage vessels. These were steeped in a mixture of vinegar, oil, and brine, sometimes honey, not unlike the pickles we make today.

EQUIPMENT

Pickles, chutneys, relishes, and mustards use readily available pieces of kitchen equipment, similar to those needed for jams and other preserves. Just a few different utensils are necessary.

Large nonmetallic bowls are preferred for brining and salting, the initial process in many pickle recipes that helps extract excess water from the vegetables. Everyday china or glass plates can be used to hold the vegetables or fruits down in the brining solution. Paper towels are required to dry the ingredients once they have been rinsed and drained in a plastic colander or sieve. Metal bowls, plates, and sieves should be avoided, particularly if they are to come into contact with vinegar, because vinegar will corrode them and give the pickle a disagreeable taste. Small stainless steel pans are ideal for heating vinegars and vinegar syrups. Chutneys and relishes are best made in a good-quality stainless steel preserving pan. Make sure it is spotless and that the pan is neither pitted nor warped. Avoid brass or copper preserving pans because the vinegar will corrode them.

If whole spices are to be added to the mixture, but need to be removed later, a piece of cheesecloth is most useful for tying them in. Use a double thickness of cheesecloth and secure to the pan handle with a long piece of string, so that the bag can be lifted out easily.

Stainless steel slotted spoons are useful for transferring pickles from their cooking liquid to jars. Wooden spoons are used for general stirring purposes. Although the ingredients, such as vinegar, sugar, and salt, used in pickles, chutneys, and relishes, are to some degree natural preservatives, using sterilized containers and lids for storage will also protect against spoilage. Make sure that glass jars are not cracked and can be made airtight with noncorrosive screw-top lids.

$\mathcal{P}$ICKLED ONIONS

INGREDIENTS

2–2¹/₂ lb pickling onions

¹/₂ cup sea salt

3 cups strained Spiced Pickling Vinegar (see recipe, page 120)

In this recipe, special pickling onions have been used, but you can use shallots instead if you prefer.

1 Trim and peel the onions, leaving a little root attached. Put them into a large nonmetallic bowl.

2 Dissolve the salt in 4¹/₂ cups water and pour over the onions. Cover with a cloth and leave to stand for 24 hours, stirring occasionally.

3 Rinse the onions in a plastic sieve or colander under cold running water. Drain well and dry on paper towels.

4 Pack the vegetables into sterilized jars to within 1 inch of the tops. Pour in the pickling vinegar to cover the onions by ¹/₂ inch. Gently tap the jars to remove the air pockets.

5 Seal the jars and label. Keep in a cool dark place for 3 weeks before using to allow the flavors to develop.

COOK'S TIP If the onions are pre-soaked in boiling water their skins will come off easier. Leave a little of the root attached so that the onions will remain whole and will not fall apart.

Makes about 4 cups

$\mathcal{P}$ICKLED HORSERADISH

INGREDIENTS

6 oz fresh horseradish

1¹/₂ cups strained Spiced Pickling Vinegar (see recipe, page 120)

scant ¹/₂ cup sugar

1 tsp sea salt

1 Peel and finely grate the horseradish, then check the amount. You should have about ¹/₂ cup grated horseradish.

2 Put the vinegar, sugar, and salt into a saucepan and bring to a boil. Stir over low heat until the sugar has completely dissolved, then boil for 2 minutes. Add the grated horseradish and simmer for 1 minute.

3 Pack the horseradish and vinegar mixture in warmed sterilized jars, to within ¹/₈ inch of the tops.

4 Seal the jars and label. Keep in a cool dark place for 1 week before using to allow the flavors to develop.

Makes about 1¹/₂ cups

$\mathcal{M}$OROCCAN PICKLED PEPPERS

INGREDIENTS

2 lb red and green bell peppers

¹/₄ cup sea salt

2 small heads of garlic

1¹/₄ cups olive oil

1¹/₄ cups white wine vinegar

1 Cut around the core of each pepper and pull it out. Quarter each pepper, scrape out the seeds, and cut away the white ribs. Sprinkle the inside of each quarter liberally with the salt.

2 Peel all the garlic cloves. Mix the olive oil and wine vinegar together. Pack the peppers and garlic, in layers, into a sterilized jar, to within 1 inch of the top.

3 Pour in the oil and vinegar mixture to cover the peppers and garlic by ¹/₂ inch.

4 Gently tap the jar to remove air pockets. Seal the jar and label. Keep in the refrigerator and use within 1–2 weeks.

Makes about 5 cups

MIXED VEGETABLE PICKLES

A variety of crisp vegetables look attractive when neatly layered in a tall jar and covered with Spiced Pickling Vinegar. Use them to create a colorful winter salad or as an accompaniment to creamy dips.

INGREDIENTS

1 lb green beans

1 lb small pickling onions

1 small cauliflower, weighing about 12 oz

12 oz zucchini

8 oz peeled carrots

^{1}/$_2$ cup sea salt

1^3/$_4$ cups strained Spiced Pickling Vinegar (see recipe, page 120)

Makes about 2 quarts

Make sure the vegetables are well covered with vinegar

1 ▲ Trim the beans and cut them into neat 1 inch lengths. Trim and peel the onions, leaving them whole, but with a little root attached so they do not fall apart. Cut the florets from the cauliflower and break into ^{1}/$_2$ inch pieces. Trim the zucchini and carrots and cut them into ^{1}/$_8$ inch thick slices.

2 ▶ Layer the vegetables with the salt in a large nonmetallic bowl. Put a plate on top to keep the vegetables lightly pressed down, and leave for 24–48 hours to draw out the excess moisture.

3 Rinse the vegetables in a plastic sieve or colander under cold running water until all the salt is washed off. Drain the vegetables well and dry on paper towels.

4 Neatly pack the vegetables in separate layers into sterilized jars, to within 1 inch of the tops.

5 ▲ Pour in the pickling vinegar to cover the vegetables by ^{1}/$_2$ inch. Gently tap the jars to remove any air pockets. Seal the jars and label. Keep in a cool dark place for at least 6 weeks before using to allow the flavors to develop.

PICKLED BABY VEGETABLES

INGREDIENTS

2$^1/_2$ lb mixed baby vegetables

$^1/_2$ cup sea salt

3$^1/_4$ cups strained Spiced
Pickling Vinegar
(see recipe, page 120)

PICKLED JERUSALEM ARTICHOKES Do not salt and
leave to stand overnight, but simmer in 2$^1/_3$ cups
salted water until tender. Drain, cool, and dry, then
continue from step 3.

*Choose baby vegetables that will retain their crispness during pickling.
Carrots, corn, and green beans are possible choices.*

1 Trim all the vegetables and peel, if necessary. Layer the
vegetables with the salt in a large nonmetallic bowl. Put a plate
on top to keep them lightly pressed down, and leave to stand
overnight to draw out the excess moisture.

2 Rinse the vegetables in a plastic sieve or colander under cold
running water. Drain well and dry on paper towels.

3 Pack the vegetables into sterilized jars, to within 1$^1/_2$ inch of
the tops. Slowly pour in the strained pickling vinegar to
cover the vegetables by $^1/_2$ inch. Gently tap the jars to remove
air pockets.

4 Seal the jars and label. Keep in a cool dark place for up to
4 weeks before using to allow the flavors to develop.

Makes about 2 quarts

DILL PICKLES WITH GARLIC

INGREDIENTS

3 large garlic cloves

10–12 cucumbers

1 bunch fresh dill

2$^1/_3$ cups water

3$^2/_3$ cups white wine vinegar

$^1/_3$ cup sea salt

2 tsp Pickling Spice
(see recipe, page 126)

1 tsp dill seeds

1 tsp whole black peppercorns

*There are many recipes for dill pickles, also sometimes called
kosher pickles. In this recipe, water is mixed with wine vinegar to
make a mild pickle. However, when water and vinegar are mixed,
the acetic acid is diluted and the preserving quality of the vinegar is
reduced. These pickles must therefore be kept in the refrigerator and
used within 2–3 months.*

1 Peel the garlic cloves and pack them into a sterilized jar with
the cucumbers and sprigs of dill.

2 Pour the water and white wine vinegar into a saucepan and
add the salt, pickling spice, dill seeds, and black peppercorns.
Bring to a boil, and boil rapidly over high heat for 3 minutes.
Leave to cool.

3 Pour the cooled mixture over the cucumbers to cover them
by $^1/_2$ inch. If there is too much liquid, add any remaining
spices to the jar and discard the excess liquid.

4 Seal the jar and label. Keep in the refrigerator for 3 weeks
before using to allow the flavors to develop.

Makes about 2 quarts

VARIATION Instead of leaving the cucumbers whole, thinly slice them
and layer them in sterilized jars with 2 peeled and sliced onions,
2 peeled garlic cloves, and the dill. Continue as for whole cucumbers.

$\mathcal{P}$ICKLED CAULIFLOWER WITH BELL PEPPERS

INGREDIENTS

2 cauliflowers

1 red bell pepper

2/3 cup sea salt

32/3 cups water

1 cinnamon stick, broken into
3 pieces

3 blades of mace

32/3 cups strained Spiced
Pickling Vinegar
(see recipe page 120)

1 Cut the florets from the cauliflower heads and discard the stalks. Put the florets into a large nonmetallic bowl. Core, seed, and dice the pepper and add to the bowl with the cauliflower.

2 Dissolve the salt in the water and pour over the vegetables. Put a plate on top to keep the vegetables submerged. Leave to stand for 24 hours.

3 Rinse the cauliflower and pepper in a plastic sieve or colander under cold running water. Drain well and dry on paper towels.

4 Pack the vegetables tightly into sterilized jars, to within 1 inch of the tops, adding a piece of cinnamon stick and a blade of mace to each jar. Pour in the spiced vinegar to cover the vegetables by 1/2 inch.

5 Seal the jars and label. Keep in a cool dark place for 4 weeks before using to allow the flavors to develop.

Makes about 4 cups

$\mathcal{Z}$UCCHINI PICKLES

INGREDIENTS

3 lb zucchini

1 lb onions

1 cup sea salt

10 cups water

13/4 cups white vinegar

1 cups sugar

2 tsp mustard seeds

1 tsp celery seeds

1 tsp whole allspice

1 Trim the zucchini and peel and trim the onions. Slice both vegetables thinly and place them in a large nonmetallic bowl.

2 Dissolve the salt in water and pour over the vegetables. Leave to stand for 3 hours, stirring occasionally.

3 Mix all the remaining ingredients in a saucepan. Stir over low heat, with a wooden spoon, until the sugar has completely dissolved.

4 Rinse the zucchini and onions in a plastic sieve or colander. Drain well and dry on paper towels. Put into a preserving pan. Pour the hot vinegar over the vegetables and leave to stand, off the heat, for 1 hour.

5 Put the pan over medium heat and bring to a boil. Boil for 3 minutes, then remove from the heat.

6 Transfer the vegetables to warmed sterilized jars, to within 1/2 inch of the tops. Pour in the vinegar to cover the vegetables by 1/2 inch. Seal the jars and label. Keep in a cool dark place for 2 weeks before using to allow the flavors to develop.

Makes about 6 cups

PICKLED BELL PEPPERS

Peppers offer a riot of color when used in making pickles. Extra flavor comes from slivers of sun-dried tomatoes and a spiced vinegar, that has a hint of sweetness. Serve these pickles with cold meats or on an antipasto *platter.*

INGREDIENTS

4 large bell peppers (red, green, orange, and yellow)

1 onion

3/4 cup sea salt

1 1/2 cups strained Spiced Pickling Vinegar (see recipe, page 120)

1/4 cup sugar

1/2 cup sun-dried tomatoes

Makes about 1 quart

1 ◄ Cut around the core of each pepper and pull it out. Halve each pepper lengthwise and scrape out the seeds. Cut away the white ribs on the inside. Cut each half lengthwise into 1/8 inch wide strips. Peel and chop the onion.

2 Layer the peppers, onion, and salt in a large nonmetallic bowl. Put a plate on top to keep the vegetables lightly pressed down, and leave, covered, for 24 hours to draw out the excess moisture. Toss the vegetables occasionally.

3 Rinse the vegetables in a plastic sieve or colander under cold running water until all the salt is washed off. Drain and dry on paper towels.

4 Pour the pickling vinegar into a small saucepan. Add the sugar and stir until the sugar has completely dissolved. Cool.

5 Put the sun-dried tomatoes in a small bowl and cover with boiling water. Leave for 5 minutes, then drain well.

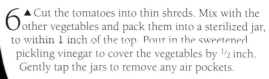

6 ▲ Cut the tomatoes into thin shreds. Mix with the other vegetables and pack them into a sterilized jar, to within 1 inch of the top. Pour in the sweetened pickling vinegar to cover the vegetables by 1/2 inch. Gently tap the jars to remove any air pockets.

7 Seal the jar and label. Keep in a cool dark place for 6 weeks before using to allow the flavors to develop.

SWEET AND SOUR CARROTS

INGREDIENTS

2 lb small carrots

1/2 cup sea salt

2 garlic cloves

1 1/4 cups white wine vinegar

1/2 cup plus 1 Tb packed dark brown sugar

2 tsp ground cinnamon

1 tsp ground coriander

1 tsp dried thyme

1 small dried red chili

These Asian-style carrots can be served on a platter of mixed hors d'oeuvre. Olives, artichoke hearts, and marinated bell peppers are excellent accompaniments.

1 Peel and thinly slice the carrots. Layer them with the salt in a large nonmetallic bowl. Put a plate on top to keep the carrots lightly pressed down, and leave, covered, for 24 hours to draw out the excess moisture. Toss the carrots occasionally.

2 Peel the garlic cloves and put them into a saucepan with all the remaining ingredients. Simmer over a low heat, stirring until the sugar has completely dissolved. Remove from the heat and leave the mixture to stand until needed.

3 Rinse the carrots in a plastic sieve or colander under cold running water until all the salt is washed off. Drain and dry on paper towels.

4 Pack the carrots into sterilized jars, to within 1 inch of the tops. Pour in the sweetened vinegar to cover the carrots by 1/2 inch. Gently tap the jars to remove air pockets.

5 Seal the jars and label. Keep in a cool dark place for 1 week before using to allow the flavors to develop.

Fills about 3 cups

PICKLED RED CABBAGE

INGREDIENTS

1 small red cabbage, weighing about 2 1/2 lb

1/3 cup sea salt

1 tsp sugar

1 1/4 cups strained Spiced Pickling Vinegar (see recipe, page 120)

1 Remove any discolored outer leaves from the cabbage. Cut the cabbage into quarters, discarding the tough and central core. Shred the cabbage finely.

2 Layer the cabbage with the salt in a large nonmetallic bowl. Put a plate on top to keep the cabbage lightly pressed down, and leave, covered, for 24 hours to draw out the excess moisture.

3 Rinse the cabbage in a plastic sieve or colander under cold running water until all the salt is washed off. Drain and dry on paper towels.

4 Pack the cabbage into sterilized jars, sprinkling with a little sugar as you go, to within 1 inch of the tops. Pour in the pickling vinegar to cover the cabbage by 1/2 inch. Gently tap the jars to remove air pockets.

5 Seal the jars and label. Keep in a cool dark place for 2–3 weeks before using to allow the flavors to develop.

Fills about 1 quart

VARIATION

A quick version of Pickled Red Cabbage can be made if the red cabbage is not salted. However, it will not remain as crisp, and must be eaten within 2–3 months.

PICKLED DICED BEETS

INGREDIENTS

2 lb uncooked beets

1 tsp sea salt

1 tsp grated horseradish
(optional)

4$\frac{1}{2}$ cups white wine vinegar

This recipe is for cubes of beets. If slices are preferred, follow the recipe as directed and, when the beets are cool, peel and slice them. Pack the slices into sterilized jars and fill with cold vinegar.

1 Wash the beets, taking care not to damage the skins.

2 Put the beets into a large saucepan and cover with water. Add the salt. Simmer for 1$\frac{1}{2}$–2 hours or until the beets are tender. Do not pierce to test or the beets will "bleed" and lose their color. Leave to cool.

3 Peel the beets, and cut into dice. Pack the diced beets into sterilized jars, with the horseradish if using, to within 1 inch of the tops.

4 Pour the vinegar into a pan and bring to a boil. Immediately pour the boiling vinegar over to beets to cover them by $\frac{1}{2}$ inch. Gently tap the jars to remove air pockets.

5 Seal the jars and label. Keep in a cool dark place for 3 weeks before using to allow the flavors to develop.

Makes about 4 cups

TANGY PICKLED MUSHROOMS

INGREDIENTS

1$\frac{1}{2}$ lb mushrooms

3 inch piece of fresh gingerroot

1 lemon

1 onion

4 cups white wine vinegar

1 Tb sea salt

1 tsp black peppercorns

Although mushrooms make a great pickle, they do not keep as long as many other vegetables. Make small amounts, keep them in the refrigerator, and eat them quickly.

1 Wipe the mushrooms with a damp cloth and trim the stalks so that they are even with the caps. Do not wash or peel them. Put the mushrooms into a saucepan.

2 Peel the gingerroot with a small sharp knife, and cut it into quarters. Pare the zest from the lemon and cut the zest into thin strips. Add the ginger and lemon strips to the mushrooms.

3 Peel and thinly slice the onion and add to the pan with all the remaining ingredients. Bring the mixture to a boil and simmer for 15–20 minutes or until the mushrooms are tender.

4 Lift the mushrooms out of the cooking liquid with a slotted spoon and pack into sterilized jars.

5 Strain the liquid, pour it back into the pan, and return to a boil. Pour it over the mushrooms to cover them by $\frac{1}{2}$ inch.

6 Seal the jars, label, and keep in the refrigerator. The mushrooms are now ready to use.

Makes about 4 cups

COOK'S TIP Use closed-capped or tiny button mushrooms for this recipe. They should be completely fresh and pure white, with pale pink gills.

Sweet Pickled Beans

INGREDIENTS

1¹/₂ lb green beans

1 Tb Pickling Spice
(see recipe, page 126)

1 lb black peppercorns

2 cups white wine vinegar

scant ¹/₂ cup sugar

1 bay leaf

1 garlic clove

1 onion

1 red bell pepper

4 large sprigs of dill

Serve pickled beans as an hors d'oeuvre or with egg salad.

1 Top and tail the beans and cut into 3 inch lengths. Put them into a pan of boiling water and boil for 1 minute. Drain, rinse under cold running water, and drain again.

2 Put the pickling spices and peppercorns on a square of cheesecloth and tie up tightly into a bag with a long piece of string. Tie the bag to the handle of a saucepan. Put the vinegar, sugar, bay leaf, and garlic clove into the saucepan.

3 Stir the mixture over a low heat, with a wooden spoon, until the sugar has completely dissolved. Bring to a boil and simmer for 10 minutes. Remove and discard the cheesecloth bag, bay leaf, and garlic clove. Leave to cool.

4 Meanwhile, peel and dice the onion. Core, seed, and dice the red bell pepper. Mix the two together and set aside.

5 Pack the beans upright into sterilized jars. Spoon in the onion and pepper mixture to within 1 inch of the tops. Add 2 sprigs of dill to each jar and slowly pour in the sweetened vinegar to cover the beans by ¹/₂ inch.

6 Seal the jars and label. Keep in a cool dark place for 2 weeks before using to allow the flavors to develop.

Makes about 2 cups

Japanese Pickled Ginger

INGREDIENTS

8 oz fresh gingerroot

sea salt

scant 1 cup rice or mild white vinegar

1 Tb sugar

a few drops of red food coloring

ORIENTAL PICKLE
Japanese Pickled Ginger, known as shoga or gari in Japan, has both a tart and sweet taste.

In Japan, pickled ginger is always served with sushi – vinegared rice garnished with raw fish and shellfish. It also goes well with other seafoods and poultry. Traditionally, fresh plum juice is used to subtly color the pickling liquid, but red food coloring works just as well.

1 Peel the gingerroot and cut it along the grain into the thinnest possible slices. Put them into a nonmetallic bowl, cover with cold water, and leave to stand for 30 minutes.

2 Drain the ginger and put it into a saucepan of boiling water. Bring back to a boil, drain again, and let cool. Return the ginger to the bowl and sprinkle lightly with salt.

3 In a saucepan, combine the vinegar and sugar. Simmer over low heat, stirring, until the sugar has completely dissolved. Stir in a few drops of red food coloring. Pour the vinegar mixture over the ginger, making sure it is completely submerged. Cover the bowl and let the ginger stand in a cool dark place for 2 weeks before using to allow the flavors to develop.

4 Transfer the ginger and liquid to a sterilized jar. Seal the jar, label, and keep in the refrigerator.

Makes about 1¹/₂ cups

FIVE-SPICE PEACHES

Bottle up the taste of summer with these juicy peaches. Spiced and enveloped in a fragrant sweet and sour syrup, they make an ideal partner for cold meats, especially pork and ham. Pack them into one large jar or two smaller ones, for individual gifts.

INGREDIENTS

4 lb peaches

2¹/₃ cups white wine vinegar

12 black peppercorns

1 tsp whole cloves

4 cardamom pods

2 cinnamon sticks

2 star anise

5 cups sugar

Makes about 1 quart

1 ◀ Bring a saucepan of water to a boil and put each peach into it for 30–40 seconds. The timing will depend on the ripeness of the fruit. Remove the peaches with a slotted spoon and transfer to a bowl of ice water. Leave to cool, then drain and dry well.

PICKING PEACHES
Select your peaches for pickling at the height of the season when their skins blush with a rosy bloom.

2 ▲ Halve the peaches, using the indentation on one side as a cutting guide. Pit and peel them. Discard the pits and skin and set the peaches aside.

3 ▶ Bring the wine vinegar and spices to a boil in a preserving pan. Add the sugar and stir, over low heat, until it has completely dissolved.

4 ▼ Boil the mixture for 2 minutes. Add the peach halves and simmer for 4–5 minutes or until the peaches are tender when pierced with a knife.

SPLENDID SPICES
Whole spices are used rather than ground ones to give the peaches a crystal-clear syrup in which to soak and mature.

FINISHING TOUCHES
Ladle the syrup right to the top of the jar so that the peaches are completely covered. If using more than one jar, make sure the spices are evenly divided between them so that all the peaches can absorb their flavor.

5 ▲ Transfer the peaches to a warmed sterilized jar, to within 1/2 inch of the top. Boil the syrup for 2–3 minutes longer until it has slightly reduced.

6 ▶ Pour syrup over the peaches. Seal the jar and label. Keep in a cool dark place for 2 months before using to allow the flavors to develop.

PICKLED CHERRIES

INGREDIENTS

7 cups white wine vinegar

1/4 cup sea salt

2 lb cherries

4 sprigs of fresh tarragon

12 black peppercorns

Ripe cherries do not keep long, so pickling provides an ideal opportunity to savor these delectable fruits.

1 Pour half of the vinegar into a saucepan and add half of the salt. Boil for 3 minutes; remove from heat and leave to cool.

2 Prick the cherries all over with a sterilized needle or a wooden toothpick. Pack into 2 sterilized jars, with 2 sprigs of tarragon and 6 peppercorns in each jar, to within 1 inch of the tops.

3 Pour in the cold salted vinegar to cover the cherries by 1/2 inch, making sure there are no air pockets. Seal the jars. Keep in a cool dark place for 1 week.

4 Repeat step 1 with the remaining vinegar and salt. Drain off the old salted vinegar from the cherries. Discard the tarragon sprigs. Pour in the fresh salted vinegar as in step 3.

5 Seal again and label. Keep in a cool dark place for 3 weeks before using to allow the flavors to develop.

Makes about 2 quarts

SPICED APPLES WITH ROSEMARY

INGREDIENTS

1 3/4 cups cider vinegar

1/2 cup honey

12 large crisp eating apples

6 sprigs of fresh rosemary

1 tsp allspice berries

This pickle is delicious served with pork, poultry, or ham, as an alternative to applesauce.

1 Pour the vinegar into a saucepan and add the honey. Stir over low heat until the honey has completely dissolved. Bring to a boil, and simmer for 2–3 minutes.

2 Peel, halve, and core the apples. Cut the apple flesh into quarters and then into eighths. Add to the pan of vinegar and honey. Simmer for 8–10 minutes or until the apples are tender but not too soft.

3 Carefully pack the apples into 3 warmed sterilized jars, to within 1 inch of the tops, adding 2 sprigs of rosemary and a few allspice berries to each jar. Pour in the vinegar mixture to cover the apples by 1/2 inch, making sure there are no air pockets. Seal the jars and label.

4 Keep in a cool dark place for 5–6 days before using to allow the flavors to develop.

Makes about 6 cups

DID YOU KNOW? Honey ranges in appearance from light and clear, to thick and opaque; the flavor depends on the flower from which the pollen came. Any commercial honey can be used in this recipe.

Spiced Oranges

INGREDIENTS

4 large seedless oranges or tangelos

2 cups sugar

1¼ cups white wine vinegar

½ tsp whole cloves

1 cinnamon stick

3 blades of mace

1 With a sharp chef's knife, cut the unpeeled oranges into slices about ¼ inch thick.

2 Put the orange slices into a saucepan and pour in enough water just to cover. Partly cover the pan with a lid and simmer for about 1 hour, or until the orange slices are soft. Remove the slices carefully and drain well in a plastic colander or sieve.

3 Combine the sugar and vinegar in a saucepan and stir over low heat until the sugar has completely dissolved. Add the spices to the syrup and boil for 5 minutes. (If you wish to remove the spices later, put them in a cheesecloth bag before adding to the sugar and vinegar.)

4 Add the orange slices to the spiced syrup. Simmer, covered, for 15–20 minutes or until the orange slices are semitransparent and the syrup is fairly thick.

5 Remove the orange slices from the spiced syrup, using a slotted spoon, and arrange neatly in 2 warmed sterilized jars, to within ½ inch of the tops. Discard the cheesecloth bag, if used. Pour the syrup and spices over the orange slices, making sure there are no air pockets.

6 Seal the jars and label. Keep in a cool dark place for 6 weeks before using to allow the flavors to develop.

Makes about 4 cups

Pickled Dates

INGREDIENTS

2 lb fresh dates

1 Tb sea salt

2⅓ cups white wine vinegar

12 black peppercorns

12 whole cloves

2 cinnamon sticks

Serve this pickle with a grilled cheese sandwich, with lamb or with grilled chicken.

1 Put the dates into a pan of boiling water. Immediately remove from the heat and leave to stand for 2 minutes. Drain and peel. Cut the dates in half lengthwise; remove and discard the pits.

2 Layer the dates with the salt in 2 sterilized jars to within 1 inch of the tops.

3 Put all the remaining ingredients into a saucepan and bring to a boil. Boil for 1 minute, then pour the mixture over the dates to cover them by ½ inch, making sure there are no air pockets between the dates.

4 Seal the jars and label. Keep in a cool dark place for 2 weeks before using to allow the flavors to develop.

Makes about 4 cups

VARIATION Adapt the recipe above to make Pickled Walnuts. First cover the nuts with a standard brine: use 2 Tb salt and 2⅓ cups water for every 1 lb shelled walnuts. Leave for 3 days. Drain and cover the walnuts with fresh brine. Leave for 1 week. Drain the walnuts and pack into sterilized jars. Boil the vinegar and spices for 1 minute, cool, and pour into the jars to cover the walnuts. Finish as directed, keeping for 5–6 weeks before using.

PICKLED PEPPERED KIWI

Chunks of tropical kiwifruit blend with apple in this exotic pickle. Very light cooking in a mildly peppered syrup ensures the texture and flavor of the fruits are preserved. Try the pickled kiwi as an unusual cooling accompaniment to hot curries.

INGREDIENTS

8 kiwifruit, total weight about 1¹/₂ lb

1 tsp green peppercorns, in brine

1 tsp mustard seeds

2¹/₃ cups clear unsweetened apple juice

1 cup sugar

²/₃ cup white wine vinegar

2 large crisp eating apples

Makes about 1 quart

1 ▶ Peel the kiwifruit. Cut each fruit lengthwise into quarters, then cut each quarter crosswise into thirds. Rinse the peppercorns in a small sieve. Drain and pat dry. Lightly crush the peppercorns and mustard seeds. Set them aside.

2 ◀ Put the apple juice and wine vinegar into a saucepan and bring to a boil. Add the sugar and stir over low heat, with a wooden spoon, until it has completely dissolved. Simmer, without stirring, for 10–15 minutes or until the syrup is slightly reduced.

3 Peel and quarter the apples, then cut out and discard the cores. Cut the flesh into pieces the same size as the kiwifruit.

4 Put the apple pieces, crushed peppercorns, and mustard seeds into the saucepan with the syrup. Stir gently to mix, being careful not to break up the apple.

5 ▲ Bring the mixture to a boil, and simmer, stirring occasionally, for 2 minutes. Add the kiwifruit and simmer for 2 minutes longer or until the fruits are just tender when pierced with a sharp knife.

6 Spoon the fruits and syrup into warmed sterilized jars, to within ¹/₈ inch of the tops. Seal the jars and label. Keep in a cool dark place for 1 week before using to allow the flavors to develop.

SPICED PICKLED PEARS

INGREDIENTS

3 lb pears

1 cinnamon stick

1 tsp allspice berries

1 tsp whole cloves

1 blade of mace

2 small pieces of peeled, dried gingerroot

1 cup sugar

2 cups cider vinegar

These aromatically spiced pears are excellent for serving with duckling, or any roasted or cold meats, poultry, and game. They are also good chopped and added to curries at the last minute.

1 Peel the pears. Quarter them if large, or halve them if small. Core the pears and put them into a saucepan with just enough water to cover. Bring to a boil, and simmer for 5 minutes.

2 Drain the pears in a plastic sieve set over a large glass measuring cup. Measure the liquid and add enough water to make $1\frac{7}{8}$ cups. Pour the liquid back into the saucepan and stir in all the remaining ingredients. Simmer for 5 minutes.

3 Add the pears to the pan and continue to simmer for 30 minutes or until the fruit is translucent.

4 Transfer the pears with a slotted spoon to a warmed sterilized jar, to within $\frac{1}{2}$ inch of the top. Pour the syrup over the pears to cover. If using more than one jar, make sure the spices are evenly divided between the jars.

VARIATION To make Spiced Pickled Apricots, first halve and pit the apricots, then proceed as for the pears. Reduce the final cooking time, cooking the apricots just until they are soft.

5 Seal the jar and label. Keep in a cool dark place for at least 1 month before using to allow the flavors to develop.

Makes about 1 quart

SPICED PRUNES WITH EARL GREY TEA

INGREDIENTS

2 lb prunes

$3\frac{2}{3}$ cups cold Earl Grey tea

$1\frac{1}{4}$ cups white wine vinegar

1 cinnamon stick

1 cup sugar

16 allspice berries

6 whole cloves

2 blades of mace (optional)

Spiced prunes are delicious with roast pork or duckling. Their aromatic liquor can also be added sparingly to sauces and casseroles.

1 Put the prunes into a large nonmetallic bowl, pour in the tea, cover, and leave to soak overnight.

2 Put the prunes and liquid into a saucepan. Bring to a boil, and simmer for 15–20 minutes or until the prunes are tender. Transfer the prunes to warmed sterilized jars, to within $\frac{1}{2}$ inch of the tops.

3 Add the vinegar to the saucepan. Break the cinnamon stick in half and add it to the saucepan with the remaining ingredients. Stir over low heat until the sugar has completely dissolved. Increase the heat and boil the syrup for 2–3 minutes or until it has reduced and thickened.

4 Pour the syrup over the prunes to cover. Make sure the spices are evenly divided between the jars.

5 Seal the jars and label. Keep in a cool dark place for at least 2 weeks before using to allow the flavors to develop.

Makes about 6 cups

DID YOU KNOW?
Earl Grey tea is a scented tea, named after the 2nd Earl Grey, for whom it was created. Earl Grey tea is a blend of China and Darjeeling teas and is delicately flavored with oil of bergamot.

CHUTNEYS

ORIGINALLY FROM INDIA, where their Hindu name, *chatni,* means "strongly spiced," chutneys are much more than that – rich concoctions of fruits, vegetables, herbs, and spices, that are slow-cooked with vinegar and sugar to produce a sweet-sour condiment. The most popular spices are the aromatic ones – cinnamon, allspice, and ginger. Mango chutney is surely the greatest favorite and is a good way to preserve the perfumed flavor of mangoes with their all-too-short season.

Chutneys can be freshly made to eat right away, but the cooked version is the most commonly known. Chutneys are an ideal side dish, and they go with almost anything. They also keep well, improving with age.

A chutney invites improvization. Although mango chutney is a classic, magnificent chutneys can be made with nectarines, peaches, pears, apricots, beets, green and red tomatoes, pineapples, and papayas – the list is almost endless. They can be very hot, if made with chilies, or mild, with their sweetness predominating. The perfect time for chutney making is when there is a glut of fruits and vegetables on the market, and there is no reason why a gifted cook should not experiment with new combinations of ingredients – dates with oranges, green tomatoes with apples, and dried apricots with almonds, are but a few of the delectable possibilities.

MAKING CHUTNEYS

❧ Select the ingredients. Chutney is perfect for using up misshapen and bruised fruits and vegetables that are not suitable for other preserves in which appearance is all important. The produce can also be riper than that used for jam making, but not overripe. Other ingredients added for flavor are spices, vinegar, dried fruits, nuts, and sugar. White sugar, or brown for its color and flavor, can be used, and so too can honey, syrup, or molasses, but in small quantities only, since they can crystallize during storage.
❧ Wash the fruits and vegetables and, if necessary, peel or skin. Chop the fruits and vegetables by hand, or in a food processor for a finer, less chunky chutney.
❧ Long slow cooking is best for chutneys so that the ingredients can break down and their flavors extracted. It may be necessary to simmer hard- or thick-skinned fruits or vegetables, such as unripe pears, carrots, or gooseberries, in vinegar first to soften them.
❧ The chutney is ready when it has a thick jamlike consistency and there is no runny vinegar visible when a spoon is drawn in a line across the bottom of the pan. Spoon the chutney into warmed sterilized jars (see page 11), to within $1/8$ inch of the tops, and stir to remove air pockets.

How to seal and store
Seal the jars very tightly with vinegar-proof lids. Metal screw tops with plastic linings are the best choice for sealing chutneys because they ensure that the vinegar does not evaporate and dry out the chutney. Although all chutneys can be eaten immediately, most are best left for about 1 month before being eaten to allow sufficient time for the flavors to develop. Chutneys generally keep for up to 1 year if stored in a cool, dry and dark place, but some chutneys have different storage times, which are given in individual recipes.

What can go wrong and why
If the chutney dries out or shrinks in the jar, it has been overboiled, not covered tightly enough, or stored in a warm place. Moldy chutney is caused by insufficient vinegar, undercooking, or the use of unsterilized jars. Liquid on the surface of a chutney is a result of insufficient boiling down of the mixture so the liquid does not evaporate.

DARK MANGO CHUTNEY

Some mango chutneys are sweet and light – but this one is mysteriously dark and spicy. No individual flavor dominates, the ingredients just all blend together in a simply delightful way.

INGREDIENTS

3 lb mangoes

2 Tb salt

1/3 cup tamarind pulp

1 6-inch piece fresh gingerroot

1/2 oz dried red chilies

2 cups cider vinegar

3 cups packed light brown sugar

2 2/3 cups raisins

1 tsp ground allspice

Makes about 5 1/2 cups

1 ◄Cut each mango on both sides of the pit; slice the flesh away from the pit and discard the pit. Peel the mango slices and cut the flesh into chunks. Put the mango flesh into a nonmetallic bowl, stir in the salt, cover, and leave for 2 hours.

2 Put the tamarind pulp into a bowl and cover it with water. Leave for 1 hour, then drain off the excess water.

3 Put the tamarind pulp into a plastic sieve set over a bowl. Press the pulp through the sieve; discard the seeds. Drain the mangoes. Rinse the mango chunks in a plastic sieve under cold running water, until all the salt is washed off. Drain well. Put the sieved tamarind pulp and the mango flesh into a preserving pan.

4 Peel and finely chop the ginger. Halve the chilies lengthwise, and remove and discard all the seeds. Either tear the chilies into small pieces with your fingers or chop them with a small knife.

MYSTERY MANGO
A delicious complement to curries, simple cheese platters, and hot or cold meats and poultry.

5 ◄Stir the ginger, chilies, vinegar, sugar, raisins, and allspice into the mango and tamarind mixture. Bring to a boil, stirring. Simmer over medium heat, stirring occasionally, for 30 minutes or until the mangoes are tender and the chutney has reduced and thickened.

6 ►Test by pulling the back of the spoon across the bottom of the pan. There should be no runny vinegar visible.

7 Spoon the chutney into warmed sterilized jars, to within 1/8 inch of the tops. Stir, if necessary, to remove air pockets. Seal the jars and label.

Autumn Fruit Chutney

INGREDIENTS

1 lb pears

1 lb cooking apples

1 lb red plums

1 medium onion

1¹/3 cups raisins

2¹/3 cups cider vinegar

finely grated zest and juice of
1 orange

2 cups packed light brown
sugar

¹/2 tsp ground
allspice

An ideal chutney to use up end-of-season fruits. Any variety of pears and plums can be used, or they can be substituted by quinces, peaches, nectarines, and apricots.

1 Core the pears and apples, without peeling them. Cut them into small chunks and put them into a preserving pan.

2 Pit the plums, and peel and chop the onion. Add them to the pan with the raisins, vinegar, and the orange zest and juice.

3 Bring the mixture to a boil, stirring. Simmer over medium heat, stirring occasionally, for about 45 minutes.

4 Add the sugar and allspice and stir over low heat until the sugar has completely dissolved. Simmer, stirring occasionally, for 1 hour or until the chutney has reduced and thickened.

5 Spoon the chutney into warmed sterilized jars, to within ¹/8 inch of the tops. Seal the jars and label. Keep in a cool dark place for 2 months before using to allow the flavors to develop.

**Makes about
6 cups**

Nectarine Chutney

INGREDIENTS

1¹/2 lb firm nectarines

1 medium onion

2 garlic cloves

1 4-inch piece of gingerroot

1¹/3 cups golden raisins

1 cinnamon stick

1 dried red chili, crushed

2 tsp salt

¹/2 tsp freshly grated nutmeg

scant 1 cup orange juice

1¹/3 cups cider or white wine
vinegar

1 Halve the unpeeled nectarines and remove the pits. Chop the flesh very coarsely. Peel and chop the onions and garlic. Peel and finely chop the ginger.

2 In a large saucepan, combine the nectarines, onion, garlic, and ginger with all the remaining ingredients. Bring to a boil, stirring. Simmer over low heat, stirring occasionally, for 40 minutes or until the chutney has reduced and thickened. Discard the cinnamon sticks.

3 Spoon the chutney into warmed sterilized jars, to within ¹/8 inch of the tops. Seal the jars and label.

Makes about 3 cups

DID YOU KNOW? There are more than 100 varieties of nectarines available, with new varieties being developed every year. The most popular varieties include "Fantasia" and "Fairlaie."

DATE AND ORANGE CHUTNEY

INGREDIENTS

1 lb dried dates

1 lb oranges

2 medium onions

4 cups sugar

1/3 cup golden syrup or 2 Tb light corn syrup with 2 Tb molasses

2 Tb sea salt

1/4 tsp dried red chilies, crushed

5 1/2 cups malt vinegar

2 2/3 cups raisins

1 Pit and chop the dates. Finely grate the zest of 2 oranges, and set aside. Remove and discard the peel, pith, and seeds from all the oranges. Finely chop the orange flesh. Peel and chop the onions.

2 Combine the sugar, golden syrup, salt, chilies, and vinegar in a preserving pan. Simmer over low heat, stirring frequently, until the sugar has completely dissolved. Bring to a boil.

3 Add the dates, oranges, onions, raisins, and half of the grated orange zest. Lower the heat and simmer, stirring occasionally, for 1 hour or until the chutney has reduced and thickened. Stir in the remaining orange zest.

4 Spoon the chutney into warmed sterilized jars, to within 1/8 inch of the tops. Seal the jars and label. Keep in a cool dark place for 2 months before using to allow the flavors to develop.

Makes about 7 1/2 cups

COOK'S TIP For a stronger orange flavor, grate the zest from all the oranges, adding half during cooking and the remainder just before spooning the chutney into the jars.

PINEAPPLE CHUTNEY

INGREDIENTS

2 pineapples with leaves removed, total weight about 2 1/4 lb

1 cup sugar

7 Tb white wine vinegar

2 tsp curry powder

1 tsp ground cinnamon

1/2 tsp ground cloves

1/2 tsp ground ginger

Lightly spiced and fruity, this chutney is ideal for serving with ham, baked Camembert, or smoked fish.

1 With a sharp knife, cut off the peel from the pineapple in strips deep enough to remove the "eyes" with the peel. Cut the pineapples into thick slices, and cut out and discard the hard central core from each slice; then dice the flesh. Set aside. Discard the peel and central core.

2 Put the sugar, vinegar, spices, and any juice from the pineapple into a preserving pan.

3 Simmer over low heat until the sugar has completely dissolved. Bring to a boil. Simmer for 5 minutes or until the syrup reduces in volume by two-thirds.

4 Add the pineapple pieces and simmer over low heat, stirring occasionally, for 20 minutes or until the pineapple is soft.

5 Spoon the chutney into warmed sterilized jars, to within 1/8 inch of the tops. Seal the jars and label.

Makes about 2 cups

RED TOMATO CHUTNEY

A mild and aromatic fruit and vegetable chutney that is made with a careful balance of spices. Let the flavors blend and mature by storing the chutney for a couple of months before eating. It is the perfect accompaniment to thick wedges of mature cheese and crusty fresh bread.

INGREDIENTS

3 lb ripe tomatoes

1 1/2 lb small onions

2 lb cooking apples

2 cups white wine vinegar

1/2 cup sugar

1 cup raisins

2 tsp salt

1 tsp ground cloves

1 tsp ground ginger

1/2 tsp cayenne pepper

Makes about 6 cups

1 ◄ Cut the cores out of the tomatoes. Put the tomatoes into a bowl and cover with boiling water. Leave for 15–20 seconds or until the skins start to split. Transfer the tomatoes to a bowl of cold water. Remove from the water one at a time and peel away the skins, using a sharp knife. Roughly chop the tomatoes.

2 ► Peel and thinly slice the onions. Peel, core, and chop the apples. Put the tomatoes, onions, and apples into a preserving pan. Add remaining ingredients and stir to combine.

3 ◄ Bring to a boil, stirring. Lower the heat and simmer, stirring often, for 40–45 minutes or until the fruit and vegetables are soft and the chutney has reduced and thickened. Test by drawing the back of the spoon across the bottom of the pan. There should be no runny liquid visible.

4 Spoon the chutney into warmed sterilized jars, to within 1/8 inch of the tops. Stir, if necessary, to remove any air pockets. Seal the jars and label. Keep in a cool dark place for 2 months before using to allow the flavors to develop.

LEMON AND MUSTARD SEED CHUTNEY

INGREDIENTS

8 large lemons, total weight about 4 lb

1 lb onions

1/4 cup salt

1 3/4 cups water

4 cups sugar

1 1/3 cups golden raisins

1/4 cup mustard seeds

2 tsp ground ginger

1 tsp cayenne pepper

3 2/3 cups cider vinegar

An excellent accompaniment for a Cheddar cheese sandwich. If the mustard seeds are omitted, the plain lemon chutney tastes good with Thai or Indian food.

1 Cut the lemons into 1/8 inch slices. Cut the slices into quarters; discard any seeds. Peel and slice the onions.

2 Layer the lemon and onion slices with the salt in a large nonmetallic bowl. Put a plate on top to keep the mixture lightly pressed down. Leave covered for 24 hours to draw out the excess moisture.

3 Rinse the lemon and onion slices in a plastic sieve or colander under cold running water until all the salt is washed off. Put them into a preserving pan and pour in water to cover. Bring to a boil. Simmer over low heat, stirring occasionally, for about 35 minutes or until the lemon peel is very tender.

4 Add the remaining ingredients and return to a boil, stirring. Simmer over low heat, stirring occasionally, for 45–50 minutes or until the chutney has reduced and thickened.

5 Spoon the chutney into warmed sterilized jars, to within 1/8 inch of the tops. Seal the jars and label. Keep in a cool dark place for 2 months before using to allow the flavors to develop.

Makes about 7 cups

PRUNE AND HAZELNUT CHUTNEY

INGREDIENTS

2 lb prunes

1 1/2 lb cooking apples

1/4 cup water

2 3/4 cups packed dark brown sugar

2 cups hazelnuts

2 1/3 cups red wine vinegar

1 tsp curry powder

1 tsp ground cinnamon

1/2 tsp ground allspice

1/4 tsp cayenne pepper

This fruity chutney does not need a long time to mature, in fact it seems to have better flavor when it is young. Serve with cold chicken or ham.

1 Put the prunes into a bowl and cover with boiling water. Leave to stand for 24 hours.

2 Peel, core, and finely chop the apples. Put them into a preserving pan with the water and 1/4 cup of the sugar. Stir over low heat until the sugar has completely dissolved. Simmer for 10 minutes or until the apples are tender.

3 Chop the nuts finely. Drain the prunes and remove the pits. Chop the prunes and add to the pan with the nuts and all the remaining ingredients. Stir to combine.

4 Bring to a boil, stirring. Simmer over low heat, stirring frequently, for 30 minutes or until the chutney has reduced and thickened.

5 Spoon the chutney into warmed sterilized jars, to within 1/8 inch of the tops. Seal the jars and label. Keep in a cool dark place for 6 weeks before using to allow the flavors to develop.

Makes about 7 cups

BANANA CHUTNEY

INGREDIENTS

3 bananas

1 lb dried dates

1/2 cup sliced candied ginger

13/4 cups white wine vinegar

finely grated zest and juice of
1 lemon and 1 orange

11/3 cups raisins

11/3 cups packed dark soft
brown sugar

2 tsp each of salt and curry
powder

1 Peel the bananas and cut them into small pieces. Pit and chop the dates, and chop the candied ginger.

2 Put the prepared ingredients into a preserving pan with the vinegar, lemon and orange zest and juice, and bring to a boil. Lower the heat and simmer, stirring occasionally with a wooden spoon, for 30 minutes.

3 Add all the remaining ingredients and stir over low heat until the sugar has completely dissolved. Return to a boil and simmer, stirring frequently, for 10–15 minutes longer or until the chutney has reduced and thickened.

4 Spoon the chutney into warmed sterilized jars, to within 1/8 inch of the tops. Seal the jars and label. Keep in a cool dark place for 1–2 months before using to allow the flavors to develop.

Makes about 3 cups

PAPAYA CHUTNEY

INGREDIENTS

2 lb unripe papaya

1 cup cashews

1 4-inch piece fresh gingerroot

3 large garlic cloves

2 fresh hot red chilies

11/3 cups golden raisins

2 cups packed light soft brown
sugar

2 cups cider vinegar

2 tsp salt

1 Peel the papaya, scrape out and discard the black seeds, and cut the flesh into 1 inch cubes.

2 Toast the cashews on a baking tray in a 350°F oven for 15 minutes or until lightly browned. Let them cool slightly, and coarsely chop. Peel and finely chop the gingerroot and the garlic cloves. Halve, seed, and chop the fresh chilies.

3 Put all the ingredients into a preserving pan. Simmer, stirring occasionally, for 30 minutes or until the chutney has reduced and thickened.

4 Spoon the chutney into warmed sterilized jars, to within 1/8 inch of the tops. Seal the jars and label. Keep in a cool dark place. The chutney can be used immediately, but it improves if stored for 2 weeks before using to allow the flavors to develop.

Makes about 31/2 cups

ORANGE CHUTNEY

INGREDIENTS

6 oranges, total weight
about 2 lb

1 medium onion

1 lb fresh dates

21/3 cups white wine vinegar

2 tsp ground ginger

2 tsp ground coriander

1 Peel the oranges, discarding the peel and seeds. Chop the flesh, and put it, with any juice, into a preserving pan.

2 Peel and chop the onions, and pit and chop the dates. Add to the pan with the oranges. Add all of the remaining ingredients and bring to a boil. Simmer, stirring occasionally, for 1 hour or until the chutney has reduced and thickened.

3 Spoon the chutney into warmed sterilized jars, to within 1/8 inch of the tops. Seal the jars and label. Keep in a cool dark place for 11/2–2 months before using to allow the flavors to develop.

Makes about 3 cups

Beet Chutney

INGREDIENTS

2 cooking apples

1 onion

1 cup malt vinegar

2 tsp freshly grated gingerroot

1 tsp ground allspice

2 whole cloves

1 lb cooked beets
(see box, right)

1/4 cup packed dark brown sugar

1/2 cup raisins

1 Core and slice the apples. Peel and slice the onion. Put the apples and onion into a preserving pan. Add the vinegar with the gingerroot, allspice, and cloves; bring to a boil. Simmer, stirring occasionally, for 20 minutes.

2 Peel the cooked beets, finely chop them, and add to the pan with the sugar and raisins. Bring to a boil and simmer for 15 minutes.

3 Spoon the chutney into warmed sterilized jars, to within 1/8 inch of the tops. Seal the jars and label. The chutney is now ready to use.

Makes about 2 1/2 cups

TO COOK BEETS Do not peel the beets before cooking because they will "bleed." Bring a pan of salted water to a boil, add the beets, and simmer for 20–30 minutes. Drain and cool.

Bengal Chutney

INGREDIENTS

3 carrots

1 onion

2 large apples

2/3 cup raisins

1/4 lb freshly grated horseradish

1 cup raw turbinado sugar

1/4 cup salt

1 Tb ground ginger

1 Tb curry powder

1 tsp mustard seeds

2 Tb cane syrup

1 1/4 cups vinegar

Chutneys are served as condiments in an Indian meal in the same way salt and pepper are in the West. This chutney comes from Bengal, in northern India.

1 Peel and slice the carrots and onion. Peel, core, and slice the apples. Put all the sliced ingredients into a saucepan.

2 Add all the remaining ingredients to the pan. Simmer, stirring occasionally, for 50 minutes or until the chutney has reduced and thickened.

3 Spoon the chutney into warmed sterilized jars, to within 1/8 inch of the tops. Seal the jars and label. Keep in a cool dark place for 6 weeks before using to allow the flavors to develop.

Makes about 3 cups

PEAR AND ONION CHUTNEY

INGREDIENTS

3 lb pears

3 medium onions

2 medium tomatoes

2 small green bell peppers

1/4 cup raisins

2 cups raw (turbinado) sugar

1 Tb salt

1/2 tsp ground cinnamon

1/4 tsp ground cloves

good pinch of cayenne pepper

3 2/3 cups white wine vinegar

It may seem unusual to mix pears, onions, tomatoes, and bell peppers, but this unlikely combination works surprisingly well. As with most chutneys, it is a delicious accompaniment to curries, other Indian dishes, and Thai food.

1 Peel, core, and dice the pears. Peel and slice the onions, and peel and chop the tomatoes. Core, seed, and chop the bell peppers. Discard all the peel, cores, and seeds.

2 Put all the prepared vegetables into a preserving pan and simmer over low heat for 20–30 minutes, or until the vegetables are soft.

3 Add all the remaining ingredients and slowly bring to a boil, stirring with a wooden spoon, until the sugar has completely dissolved. Simmer, stirring occasionally, for 1–1 1/2 hours or until the chutney has reduced and thickened.

4 Spoon the chutney into warmed sterilized jars, to within 1/8 inch of the tops. Seal the jars and label. Keep in a cool dark place for about 2 months before using to allow the flavors to develop.

Makes about 7 1/2 cups

RHUBARB CHUTNEY

INGREDIENTS

1 lb rhubarb

1 1/2 medium onions

1 cup raisins

4 cups packed light brown sugar

2 cups cider vinegar

1 Tb salt

1 tsp ground cinnamon

1 tsp ground ginger

1/2 tsp ground cloves

pinch of cayenne pepper

1 Trim and slice the rhubarb. Peel and slice the onions.

2 Put the rhubarb and onions into a stainless steel preserving pan with all the remaining ingredients.

3 Stir over low heat, with a wooden spoon, until the sugar has completely dissolved. Bring to a boil. Simmer, stirring frequently, for 2 hours or until the chutney has reduced and thickened.

4 Spoon the chutney into warmed sterilized jars, to within 1/8 inch of the tops. Seal the jars and label.

Makes about 7 cups

COOK'S TIP Always prepare rhubarb properly before cooking – top and tail the rhubarb and peel off any tough strings if necessary. Be sure to remove all the leaves, which are poisonous and should never be eaten. Always use a stainless steel pan when cooking rhubarb because the acidity of the rhubarb may react with other metals.

SPICED BELL PEPPER CHUTNEY

INGREDIENTS

6 red bell peppers

6 green bell peppers

4 medium green or unripe tomatoes

3 medium onions

3 large (1½ lb) cooking apples

2 cups sugar

2 Tb salt

1 tsp ground allspice

3 cups cider vinegar

10 small dried red chilies

1 tsp whole cloves

½ inch piece fresh gingerroot, grated

4 tsp mustard seeds

¼ cup peppercorns

This chutney is both colorful and flavorful when served as an accompaniment to a cheese platter.

1 Halve the bell peppers and the tomatoes, and remove and discard the cores and seeds. Peel the onions and peel and core the apples. Coarsely chop all the vegetables and the apples in a food processor, or chop them roughly with a large knife.

2 Put the vegetables and fruit into a preserving pan with the sugar, salt, allspice, and vinegar. Add all the remaining ingredients, tied together tightly in a cheesecloth bag. Stir over low heat, with a wooden spoon, until the sugar has completely dissolved. Simmer, stirring occasionally, for 1¼ hours, or until the mixture has reduced and thickened.

3 Remove the cheesecloth bag, and spoon the chutney into warmed sterilized jars, to within ⅛ inch of the tops. Seal the jars and label. Keep in a cool dark place for 6 weeks before using to allow the flavors to develop.

Makes about 2 quarts

DID YOU KNOW? Bell peppers are native to tropical America and the West Indies. Bell peppers are mild in taste and can be eaten raw or cooked. Chilies or hot peppers are used as a seasoning, but don't be fooled by the green ones, which are often more fiery than red chilies.

APRICOT AND ALMOND CHUTNEY

INGREDIENTS

1 cup cider vinegar

1 cup sugar

12 apricots

2 red bell peppers

2 onions

1 garlic clove

1 orange

1 lemon

½ cup sliced candied ginger

1 tsp salt

½ cup raisins

½ cup whole blanched almonds

1 tsp ground ginger

1 Pour ¾ cup of the vinegar into a preserving pan. Add the sugar. Stir over low heat until the sugar has completely dissolved. Increase the heat and bring the mixture to a boil. Simmer for 5 minutes.

2 Halve, pit, and chop the apricots. Core, seed, and chop the bell peppers. Peel and chop the onions and garlic. Finely chop the whole orange and lemon, including the peel and pith. Finely chop the candied ginger.

3 Add the prepared fruits and vegetables to the vinegar mixture together with the candied ginger, salt, and raisins. Simmer over medium heat, stirring frequently, for 30 minutes.

4 Add the almonds, ground ginger, and remaining vinegar. Simmer for 30 minutes longer, stirring frequently, or until the chutney has reduced and thickened.

5 Spoon the chutney into warmed sterilized jars, to within ⅛ inch of the tops. Seal the jars and label. Keep in a cool dark place for at least 2 months before using to allow the flavors to develop.

Makes about 1 quart

RELISHES

WITH THEIR SPICY TANG and crisp texture, relishes provide a challenge to the cook who can choose either to follow the excellent example of tradition or to abandon the past and make creative forays into new culinary territory. Either way, the results are bound to embellish the dishes they supplement. Fine relishes are as important as a fine sauce and deserve as much attention. They are usually combinations of fruits, sweet or tart, and crisp vegetables, such as celery, radishes, carrots, and sweet bell peppers, and they complement both hot and cold meats, fish, and rich poultry especially duck and goose. Relishes are delicious with cottage cheese or ricotta as an appetizer or a light luncheon dish. They can be stirred into mayonnaise for a salad dressing, they are good in sandwiches, and give meatloaves an extra sweet-and-sour or hot chili flavor.

Most ingredients for relishes are available all year round, with the exception of that great favorite, Corn Relish, which has to be made with kernels from fresh corn cobs during the brief corn season.

There is a temptation to sample relishes to oblivion: just a taste here, a taste there, and the jar is empty. Always make enough for the pantry or refrigerator and plenty for gift giving.

MAKING RELISHES

❦ Choose young fresh fruits or vegetables. If using vegetables with a high water content, such as cabbages, cucumbers, and sweet peppers, layer them with sea salt and leave overnight to draw out the moisture.

❦ Drain the vegetables and rinse under cold running water to wash off the extra salt, drain again, and pat dry with paper towels.

❦ Cook the relish in a preserving pan with your choice of vinegar, sugar, and spices. The fruits and vegetables are cooked until they are just tender. Relishes are distinct from chutneys in that they are more coarsely textured with a sharper flavor, while chutneys are characteristically smooth and mellow. For this reason, relishes require less cooking than chutneys.

❦ Spoon the relish into warmed sterilized jars (see page 11), to within ⅛ inch of the tops and stir, if necessary, to remove air pockets.

How to seal and store

Seal the jars very tightly with noncorrosive screw-top lids and label. Store in a cool dark place for 2–4 weeks before using to allow the flavors to develop. The relishes should then keep for about 3 months, depending on the ingredients. It is a good idea to date the relishes so that it is clear when they should be used up. Once the jars of relish have been opened, keep them, tightly sealed, in the refrigerator.

What can go wrong and why

If the relish shrinks in the jar, the seal is not airtight. Relishes will lack flavor and a sharp taste if they are not left to mature for long enough before using, or if a poor-quality vinegar has been used. If the color of the relish fades, it has been exposed to light, which hastens oxidation and destroys certain vitamins.

Corn Relish

At the height of summer, when gardens and farmers' markets are overflowing with fresh ears of corn, it's time to make this traditional tangy relish. It can be eaten immediately or tucked into a cabinet to enjoy in the winter months.

Ingredients

8 fresh ears of corn, total weight about 5½ lb

2 each of red bell peppers, green bell peppers, and onions

8 celery ribs

4½ cups cider vinegar

½ cup sugar

1 Tb mustard seeds

1 Tb salt

4 allspice berries

Makes about 11 cups

1 ▶ Remove and discard the husks and silks from the fresh ears of corn.

2 ◀ Cut the corn kernels from each cob. Cut around the core of each bell pepper, and pull it out. Halve each pepper lengthwise and scrape out the seeds. Cut away the white ribs on the inside. Cut each pepper half lengthwise into strips and then crosswise into dice.

3 ▶ Peel and finely chop the onions. Finely chop the celery. Put all the vegetables into a preserving pan. Add all the remaining ingredients to the pan and stir over low heat until the sugar has completely dissolved.

4 ◀ Bring the mixture to a boil, stirring. Simmer stirring occasionally, for 15–20 minutes or until the vegetables are tender.

5 ▲ Spoon into warmed sterilized jars, to within ⅛ inch of the tops. Seal and label. The relish is now ready to use.

Horseradish Relish

INGREDIENTS

4 lb tomatoes

4 celery ribs

4 onions

8 oz grated horseradish

$1^2/_3$ cups packed brown sugar

$2^1/_3$ cups cider vinegar

2 Tb salt

2 tsp each of ground allspice, cinnamon, and cloves

$^1/_4$ cup mustard seeds

2 Tb dill seeds

1 Peel, and chop the tomatoes. Put into a plastic sieve and leave to drain for 2 hours. Chop the celery and peel and chop the onions.

2 Put the vegetables into a heavy saucepan. Add all the remaining ingredients. Stir over low heat, with a wooden spoon, until the sugar has completely dissolved. Bring to a boil and simmer, stirring occasionally, for 50 minutes or until the vegetables are soft and tender. Spoon the relish into warmed sterilized jars, seal, and label. Keep in a cool dark place for 2 months before using to allow the flavors to develop.

Makes about 10 cups

COOK'S TIP To prepare fresh horseradish, peel the skin down to the flesh with a vegetable peeler or small sharp knife. Grate or shred in a food processor (using a hand grater can produce very strong fumes, causing burning and watering eyes).

Jerusalem Artichoke Relish

INGREDIENTS

$4^1/_2$ lb Jerusalem artichokes

4 onions

2 green or red sweet bell peppers

1 Tb sea salt

1 tsp each of dill and mustard seeds, and turmeric

$^1/_2$ tsp cayenne pepper

6 cups cider vinegar

1 Peel the artichokes and onions. Core and seed the bell peppers. Coarsely mince the vegetables in a food processor, then put into a preserving pan. Add all the remaining ingredients and stir over low heat until the sugar has completely dissolved. Bring to a boil and simmer, stirring occasionally, for 30 minutes or until the vegetables are tender.

2 Spoon the relish into warmed sterilized jars. Seal the jars and label. Keep in a cool dark place for 1 week before using to allow the flavors to develop.

Makes about 10 cups

DID YOU KNOW? The Jerusalem artichoke bears no relation to the globe artichoke, but is in fact a member of the sunflower family. It has a rather odd shape and texture, but its flavor is sweet and nutty.

Cranberry-Orange Relish

INGREDIENTS

1 lb cranberries

1 cup sugar

2 oranges

Unlike other relishes, this relish does not need cooking, so it is quick and easy to prepare.

1 Chop the cranberries and put them into a nonmetallic bowl with the sugar. Stir to mix thoroughly.

2 Slice the unpeeled oranges and remove the seeds. Finely chop the orange slices in a food processor, and add them to the bowl of cranberries and sugar.

3 Spoon the relish into sterilized jars. Seal, label, and refrigerate immediately. The relish should be chilled for several hours before serving. It will keep for about 1 week in the refrigerator.

Makes about 6 cups

CARROT AND CUCUMBER RELISH

INGREDIENTS

2 large carrots

1 medium onion

6 cucumbers

1 green bell pepper

1 red bell pepper

2 small fresh green chilies

3/4 cup sea salt

3/4 cup plus 1 Tb cider vinegar

3/4 cup sugar

1 tsp mustard seeds

1 tsp fennel seeds

This appetizing relish is a great favorite. It is good with any cold meats or chicken, hamburgers, barbecued meats, or quiches. Once the jars have been opened, keep them in the refrigerator.

1 Peel and coarsely grate the carrots. Peel and finely chop the onions. Finely dice the cucumbers. Core, seed, and chop the peppers and chilies.

2 Layer the vegetables with the salt in a large nonmetallic bowl. Leave to stand overnight to draw out excess moisture.

3 Drain the vegetables and rinse in a plastic sieve or colander under cold running water, until all the salt is washed off. Drain again and dry on paper towels.

4 Combine all the remaining ingredients in a saucepan and bring to a boil. Add the drained vegetables and simmer for 10 minutes or until the vegetables are tender.

5 Spoon the relish into warmed sterilized jars. Seal the jars and label. Keep in a cool dark place for 2 weeks before using to allow the flavors to develop.

Makes about 5 cups

END-OF-SEASON RELISH

INGREDIENTS

2 medium green or unripe tomatoes

1 medium ripe tomato

1/2 small green cabbage

2 red bell peppers

2 green bell peppers

2 celery ribs

2 onions

1/2 cucumber

5 Tb sea salt

1 cup packed light soft brown sugar

2 3/4 cups cider or white wine vinegar

This is an excellent relish for using up excess garden produce left at the end of the summer. It is good with meat and poultry and with a sharply flavored cheese, such as a mature Cheddar.

1 Chop the tomatoes and cabbage coarsely. Cut around the core of each bell pepper and pull it out. Halve each pepper lengthwise and scrape out the seeds. Cut away the white ribs on the inside, and dice the peppers coarsely. Chop the celery, and peel and chop the onions. Peel and chop the cucumber.

2 Layer the vegetables with the salt in a large nonmetallic bowl. Leave to stand overnight to draw out excess moisture.

3 Drain the vegetables, pressing them to remove as much liquid as possible. Rinse in a plastic sieve under cold running water, drain again, and pat dry on paper towels. Put the vegetables into a large saucepan. Add the sugar and vinegar; stir to mix. Simmer the mixture for 1 hour or until the vegetables are tender.

4 Spoon the relish into warmed sterilized jars. Seal the jars and label. Keep in a cool dark place for 2 weeks before using to allow the flavors to develop.

Makes about 9 cups

Mustards

MUSTARD HAS BEEN cultivated since 4,000 BC; it is a versatile plant and is one of the most popular food flavorings in the world. There are huge numbers of mustard recipes, all based on three types of seed, the *nigra* (black), *juncea* (brown), and *alba* (white or yellow). Mustard seasoned the food of the ancient Egyptians, Greeks, and Romans, and is as prolific as it is ancient: a seed of black mustard can produce 3,400 young plants, making it a Hindu symbol of fertility. The name comes from the Latin *mustum ardens* or "burning must," which refers to the pungent taste that develops when the seeds are ground with must, or unfermented grape juice. Back in AD 800, the Emperor Charlemagne noted that the leaves of the mustard plant could be eaten either raw or cooked; today it is a popular vegetable in India, China, Japan, Africa, and parts of the United States. Mustard turns up in every kind of food, from appetizers, soups, sauces, and pickles, through fish, game, and meat, to vegetables and salads and even desserts and puddings.

Mustard is a member of the cabbage family, and its seeds are classified as mild to strong. The simplest form of mustard is dry mustard powder, which is a mix of ground seeds, very hot, and a favorite in England, China, and Japan. There are also whole-grain mustards, and specialty mustards, such as Dijon, German, American, Beaune, Bordeaux, and Beaujolais, that vary in taste because of the proportions of seeds ground with vinegar, sugar, and spices. Mustards can be flavored with herbs, horseradish, lemon, chili, and honey, to name just a few, and each flavor gives a delectably different taste to the mustard.

Making Mustards

❧ Select the type of seeds and flavorings. Basic mustards can be mild or strong, smooth or coarse, and the variety of seeds you use will determine the taste. White or yellow seeds are mild, black seeds are strong and pungent, and brown seeds are hot and aromatic. If you want to make a flavored mustard, use commercially ground dry mustard powder as a base, for a really smooth texture. Alternatively, for a rougher texture, grind your own seeds in an electric blender or a mortar and pestle.

❧ Add the flavorings, either aromatic fresh herbs such as tarragon and basil, hot spices like green peppercorns and crushed dried chilies, or fruits from sharp citrus to sweet berries. Even freshly grated gingerroot or horseradish can also be used. A sweetener, such as superfine sugar or honey, can be added. Vinegar is used to blend the ingredients. Whiskey or ale can also be stirred in.

❧ Spoon the mustard into sterilized jars (see page 11).

Traditional mustard pots have small necks; these keep mustard fresh for a long time, because they prevent a large surface area from coming into contact with the air.

How to seal and store
Seal the jars tightly with noncorrosive screw tops, and keep in a cool dark place for about 1–2 weeks before using to allow the flavors to develop. Use the mustard within 3 months. Once opened, the flavor will start to deteriorate, so refrigerate and use it up fairly quickly.

What can go wrong and why
If the mustard dries out on the surface, it has not been sealed correctly. If the mustard is kept for too long, it will lose most of its strength.

Whole-Grain Mustard

INGREDIENTS

2/3 cup whole black or brown mustard seeds

3/4–1 cup white wine vinegar

1/3 cup whole yellow mustard seeds

1 Tb salt

1 Put the black or brown mustard seeds into a nonmetallic bowl and pour 2/3 cup of the vinegar over. Cover and leave overnight.

2 The next day, use a mortar and pestle to pound the mixture until the seeds are coarsely broken. Grind the yellow mustard seeds in an electric grinder to a very fine powder. Combine the two mixtures and stir in the rest of the vinegar and the salt.

3 Spoon into sterilized jars. Seal, label, and keep in a cool dark place for 2 weeks before using to allow the flavors to develop.

Makes about 2 cups

Tarragon Mustard

INGREDIENTS

about 1/2 cup fresh tarragon

1/2 cup all-purpose flour

1 cup dry mustard

2 Tb superfine sugar

4 tsp salt

7 Tb white wine vinegar

1 Strip the tarragon leaves from their stalks. Discard the stalks and finely chop the leaves.

2 Sift the flour into a bowl, add the mustard powder, superfine sugar, and salt. Mix the ingredients together well. Add the tarragon, and vinegar to the bowl and stir the mixture until a smooth paste forms.

3 Spoon the mustard into sterilized jars. Seal the jars and label. Keep in a cool dark place for 1 week before using to allow the flavors to develop.

Makes about 2 cups

VARIATIONS

Other flavorings can enhance the taste of mustards. Omit the fresh tarragon in this recipe and add different herbs, such as basil, parsley, mint, sage, thyme, or rosemary.

English Mustard

INGREDIENTS

2/3 cup whole yellow mustard seeds

2 Tb all-purpose plain flour

1 Tb salt

3/4 cup light ale or water

1 Put the mustard seeds in an electric grinder and grind to a fine powder. Transfer to a bowl, and sift in the flour and salt. Mix together well. Gradually beat in the ale to make a smooth paste.

2 Spoon the mustard into sterilized jars. Seal the jars and label. Keep in a cool dark place for 2 weeks before using to allow the flavors to develop.

Makes about 1 1/3 cups

Horseradish Mustard

INGREDIENTS

1/2 cup all-purpose plain flour

1 cup dry mustard

2 1/4 Tb superfine sugar

4 tsp salt

3 oz fresh horseradish

3/4 cup cider vinegar

1 Sift the flour into a bowl, add the remaining dry ingredients, and mix together well.

2 Peel and finely grate the horseradish. Add to the dry ingredients with the vinegar and mix again, to make a smooth paste.

3 Spoon the mustard into sterilized jars. Seal the jars and label. Keep in a cool dark place for 1 week before using to allow the flavors to develop.

Makes about 2 cups

Luxurious Oils & Vinegars

FLAVORED OILS

INFUSING OILS with a single flavor or a compatible combination of herbs and spices is a lovely way to make personalized gifts for friends. Almost any herb or spice can be used, along with aromatic fruit, such as oranges, lemons, or limes. Flowering herbs, such as rosemary and thyme, added to the finished bottles create a pretty effect.

Today's cooks have a wide choice of oils to work from, each with a special flavor of its own. Everyday oils – corn, canola, safflower, and sunflower – are guaranteed not to dominate the taste of the ingredients with which they are combined; these oils are generally suitable for infusing with the more pungent herbs and spices. Luxury oils, including walnut and hazelnut, and the exotics, such as mustard oil used in Indian cooking, and the bright orange, nutty palm oil used in Brazilian cooking – already have their own distinctive tastes and are not usually chosen for making flavored oils. The greatest of all the oils for flavoring is olive, and the best quality is extra-virgin olive oil, made from the first cold pressing of the finest olives.

Flavored oils can be used in marinades, salad dressings, or for the initial sauté in a stir-fry; in fact, for any dish in which you would use an ordinary oil. Simply ensure that the taste of the oil complements the ingredients you are using.

MAKING FLAVORED OILS

❦ Start by sterilizing glass bottles (see page 11). It is best to choose a small size, because oils can turn rancid after opening and small amounts will be used more quickly.
❦ Select your flavorings. If you are using herbs, they should be freshly picked and lightly dried on paper towels to remove excess moisture, then bruised lightly (see box, page 107) to release their aroma immediately. Dried spices, such as cinnamon sticks, peppercorns, and chilies, should be as fresh as possible so that their maximum flavor is extracted. Fresh garlic cloves lend pungency, but should only be used in small amounts. If garlic is added to flavor the oil, it is important to keep the oil refrigerated and to use it within 2 weeks.
❦ Insert the prepared flavorings into the bottles, then pour in the oil to fill and cover all the ingredients (so mold cannot grow). Seal the bottles.
❦ Leave for about 2 weeks in a cool dark place. During this time the flavor will develop in the oil, so taste it occasionally to see when it is ready to use. Shake the bottle a few times, especially if it contains ingredients, such as paprika that settle on the bottom. If you prefer the flavor not to get any stronger at this stage, or if you want

the oil to last longer (particularly if it contains fresh ingredients), strain it through a double layer of cheesecloth into freshly sterilized bottles. For decoration and easy identification, a fresh herb sprig can be added to herb oils, or a twist of orange or lemon zest to citrus oils.

How to seal and store
Seal tightly in bottles with noncorrosive screw-top lids, label, then keep in the refrigerator for 3–6 months. The storage time will depend on the flavoring of the oil. Those that contain fresh ingredients, such as herbs or fruits, unless strained first, will only last about 3 months. Oils that have been infused with dried ingredients will last about 6 months.

What can go wrong and why
A flavored oil will become cloudy if its flavoring, such as fresh onions, contains too much water. If this happens, use up the oil as soon as possible, because it can quickly become rancid. Other reasons for an oil turning rancid are incorrect storage, faulty sealing of bottles, and the oil coming into contact with direct sunlight and heat.

FIERY CHILI OIL

Brilliant red chilies, infused in warm oil, produce a glowing color and potent taste that can be diluted by using fewer chilies than suggested here or by taking out the chili seeds. Use chili oil to sauté onions and garlic for stir-fries, sauces, casseroles, or soups, or mix it with vinegar to make a simple salad dressing. It will give every dish an instant burst of flavor.

INGREDIENTS

12 dried red chilies

2 cups canola oil or corn oil

1½ Tb ground cayenne pepper

2 Tb roasted sesame oil

Makes about 2 cups

1 ◄ Finely chop the chilies. Put them into a medium saucepan and pour in the canola or corn oil. Simmer over a very low heat for 10 minutes. (Do not let the oil get too hot; overheating will spoil its keeping qualities.) Remove from the heat and cool.

2 ◄ Stir in the cayenne pepper and the sesame oil. Cover the pan and leave for 12 hours to allow the flavors to develop.

3 ► Line a funnel with a double layer of cheesecloth and strain the flavored oil through it into a sterilized bottle, to within ⅛ inch of the top.

4 If you like, add 2–3 whole dried red chilies. Seal the bottle and label. The oil is now ready to use.

IDENTIFICATION PARADE
Two or three dried chilies added to the bottle of oil will make it readily identifiable on the kitchen shelf.

COOK'S TIP When chilies are lightly cooked in oil, their flavor is released instantly, so the oil can be used right away rather than left for 1–2 weeks to allow the flavors to develop.

ANNATTO OIL

INGREDIENTS

3 Tb annatto seeds

1 cup canola oil or corn oil

This oil, known in Spanish as aceite de achiote, *can be used to sauté fish, shellfish, poultry, and vegetables.*

1 Put the annatto seeds and oil into a small saucepan. Simmer over low heat, stirring occasionally, for 1–5 minutes or until the mixture turns a rich orange as the seeds give up their color. The time needed depends on the freshness of the seeds. As soon as the color of the oil begins to lighten from orange to gold, remove the pan from the heat and leave to cool.

2 Line a funnel with a double layer of cheesecloth and strain the flavored oil through it into a sterilized bottle, to within $1/8$ inch of the top.

3 Seal the bottle and label. The oil is now ready to use.

Makes about 1 cup

DID YOU KNOW?
Tiny triangular annatto seeds come from the flowering annatto tree, which grows in the Caribbean, and Central and South America. They turn oil a golden orange color, and give it a subtle spicy flavor.

SWEET PAPRIKA OIL

INGREDIENTS

4 Tb sweet paprika

3 cups extra-virgin olive oil

DO-IT-YOURSELF FUNNEL
A handmade funnel is useful for spooning ground spices into bottles. Make it with paper or foil.

1 Divide the paprika equally between sterilized bottles: spoon it through a handmade paper funnel placed in the neck of each of the bottles.

2 Pour the extra-virgin olive oil into the bottles, to within $1/8$ inch of the tops.

3 Seal the bottles and shake well. Keep in a cool dark place for 1 week before using to allow the flavors to develop. Shake the bottles occasionally.

4 Line a funnel with a double layer of cheesecloth and strain the flavored oil through it into freshly sterilized bottles. Seal and label. The oil is now ready to use.

Makes about 3 cups

ORANGE AND CORIANDER OIL

INGREDIENTS

2 Tb coriander seeds

4 strips of dried orange zest (see box, right)

3 cups extra-virgin olive oil

1 Lightly crush the coriander seeds in a mortar and pestle, being careful not to break them up completely. Alternatively, use the end of a rolling pin to crush them. Divide the coriander seeds equally between sterilized bottles.

2 If necessary, cut the dried orange zest to a size that will fit through the necks of the bottles, and add to the coriander. Pour in the oil, to within $1/8$ inch of the tops.

3 Seal the bottles and shake well. Label and keep in a cool dark place for 1 week before using to allow the flavors to develop. Shake the bottles occasionally.

Makes about 3 cups

COOK'S TIP
To dry orange zest: preheat the oven to 200°F. Peel 4 wide strips of zest from top to bottom of an orange. Put the strips on a baking tray and leave in the oven for about $1 1/4$ hours, or until dry.

MIXED HERB OIL

INGREDIENTS

2 sprigs of fresh rosemary

2 sprigs of fresh thyme

2 baby onions

2 bay leaves

12 black peppercorns

3 cups extra-virgin olive oil

1 Lightly bruise the rosemary and thyme to release their flavors. Peel and finely slice the onions.

2 Divide the bruised herbs, onion slices, bay leaves, and peppercorns equally between sterilized bottles.

3 Pour in the oil, to within ⅛ inch of the tops, making sure that the ingredients are completely covered.

4 Seal the bottles and shake well. Label and keep in a cool dark place for 2 weeks before using to allow the flavors to develop. Shake the bottles occasionally.

Makes about 3 cups

PERFUMED THAI OIL

INGREDIENTS

4–6 sprigs of fresh coriander

6 pieces of fresh lemon grass

4 dried red chilies

3 cups canola oil or corn oil

1 Lightly bruise the coriander and lemon grass with the flat side of a chef's knife, to release their flavors.

2 Divide the bruised coriander and lemon grass, and the chilies, equally between sterilized bottles. Pour in the oil, to within ⅛ inch of the tops.

3 Seal the bottles and shake well. Label and keep in a cool dark place for 2 weeks before using to allow the flavors to develop. Remove the coriander and lemon grass after 2 weeks.

Makes about 3 cups

INDIAN SPICE OIL

INGREDIENTS

1 tsp aromatic garam masala (see recipe, page 125)

½ tsp garlic powder

½ tsp ground coriander

½ tsp ground cumin

½ tsp chili powder

½ tsp ground turmeric

2 tsp dried fenugreek leaves

2 whole cloves

3 cups canola oil or corn oil

This powerfully flavored oil adds a tang to marinated or sautéed food, and is also ideal for barbecued steak and chicken.

1 Put all the powdered spices into a small bowl and mix well together. Divide the spice mixture equally between 2 sterilized bottles by spooning them through a funnel placed in each bottle neck. Divide the fenugreek leaves and cloves between the bottles.

2 Pour in the oil, to within ⅛ inch of the tops. Seal the bottles and shake well. Keep in a cool dark place for 1–2 weeks before using to allow the flavors to develop. Shake the bottles occasionally.

3 Line a funnel with a double layer of cheesecloth and strain the oil through it into 2 freshly sterilized bottles. Seal and label. The oil is now ready to use.

Makes about 3 cups

From left to right, *Perfumed Thai Oil, Sweet Paprika Oil, and Mixed Herb Oil*

OIL OF ITALY

INGREDIENTS

4 fresh sage leaves

4–6 sprigs of fresh basil

12 black or white peppercorns

4 cups extra-virgin olive oil

Italian cooks adore the earthy taste of sage and the semi-sweet flavor of basil, both of which are combined in this oil. Use it for tossing with pasta, or for drizzling over a mozzarella cheese and tomato salad.

1 Lightly bruise the herbs to release their flavor. Divide the bruised herbs and the peppercorns equally between sterilized bottles. Pour in the olive oil, to within $1/8$ inch of the tops of the bottles.

2 Seal the bottles and shake well. Label and keep in a cool dark place for 2 weeks before using to allow the flavors to develop. Shake the bottles occasionally.

Makes about 1 quart

PROVENÇAL OIL

INGREDIENTS

2 Tb mixed fresh herbs and spices, e.g. fennel stalks, oregano, tarragon, thyme, rosemary, coriander seeds, 1 bay leaf, and 1 dried red chili

2 cups extra-virgin olive oil

An intriguing mix of herbs and spices goes into this oil, which takes on the scent of southern France as it soaks up their flavors. The herbs and spices listed here are just one suggestion, but you can experiment with other combinations.

1 Put the herbs and spices into a sterilized bottle. Pour in the olive oil, to within $1/8$ inch of the top of the bottle, making sure the herbs are completely covered.

2 Seal the bottle and shake well. Label and keep in a cool dark place for 2 weeks before using to allow the flavors to develop. Shake the bottle occasionally.

Makes about 2 cups

ROSEMARY OIL

INGREDIENTS

4–6 large sprigs of fresh rosemary

4 cups extra-virgin olive oil

This is the simplest of flavored oils. Any other single herb can be used to flavor oil in the same way: lemon balm, tarragon, marjoram, oregano, mint, or thyme. For a stronger flavor, add extra herb sprigs and keep for longer before opening.

1 Bruise the rosemary (see box, below) to release its flavor.

2 Divide the sprigs of rosemary equally between sterilized bottles. Pour in the olive oil, to within $1/8$ inch of the tops of the bottles, making sure the rosemary is completely covered.

3 Seal the bottles and shake well. Label and keep in a cool dark place for 2 weeks before using to allow the flavors to develop. Shake the bottles occasionally.

Makes about 1 quart

DID YOU KNOW? To extract the full flavor from fresh herbs, it is best to bruise them just before using. Put the herbs on a chopping board and lay a large chef's knife on top of them. Using the palm of your hand, press down firmly on the flat of the knife.

PRESERVES IN OIL

OLIVE OIL, richly aromatic and fruity, is wonderful as a preserver of foods. In the commercial world, artichoke hearts, anchovies, sardines, and tuna are all traditionally preserved in olive oil. We may take them for granted, yet those of us addicted to the sharp, salty flavor of anchovies in a Caesar salad, or chunks of tuna tossed in a *salade Niçoise* would greatly miss these treats if there were no oil to preserve them for us.

There are many gifts to be made at home, using a variety of foods with oil as a preservative. Olives, mushrooms, feta and goat cheeses, and lemons will all be transformed once bathed and soaked in oil. Pack them in your favorite jars, jazz them up with fresh herbs and spices to coax out their flavors, add oil, and you will have luxurious delicacies for serving with salads, as appetizers, or as accompaniments. Sun-dried tomatoes also gain extra flavor when they are packed in oil. The concentrated tomato taste will always brighten up the topping on a pizza, the filling in a quiche, or the sauce over pasta. There is an added advantage to be gained from this process. At the same time as being kept fresh by the oil, the preserved ingredients used impart their delicious flavor to it. So, once they have been eaten, the flavored oil can be used for cooking and in salad dressings.

PRESERVES IN OIL

❧ Select the oil. The choice will depend on how strong you want the flavor to be. Ordinary olive oil is much milder in flavor than extra-virgin olive oil. Corn oil or canola oil can be used if a neutrally flavored oil is required. Nut oils are not a good choice because they tend to turn rancid much more quickly than other oils.

❧ Choose the ingredients. Vegetables can be preserved in oil, but use only those that can be processed in some way first to remove their excess water. The most common methods are salting, such as for salt-cured olives and lemons, and drying, for vegetables like mushrooms or tomatoes. Mushrooms can also be cooked to extract their moisture. Feta and goat cheeses take well to being preserved in olive oil and, after the cheese has been eaten, you can use the cheese-flavored oil for cooking or in salad dressings. Once you have chosen which foods to preserve, marry them with some scented herb sprigs or pungent spices to enhance their natural flavors.

❧ Pack the chosen ingredients and any seasonings into dry sterilized jars (see page 11), then pour in the oil almost to fill the jars and completely cover the ingredients.

❧ Leave for 1 week in a cool dark place, so that the oil can preserve and flavor the ingredients and the ingredients

flavor the oil. The longer you leave them, the more potent the taste.

How to seal and store
Seal tightly in jars with noncorrosive screw-top lids. Choose a cool dark place for storage or store in the refrigerator. Foods preserved in oil will then keep for up to 3 months. Any foods preserved in oil that contains garlic, should always be stored in the refrigerator, and used within 1–2 weeks. You must make sure that the contents of all the jars are always well covered with oil.

What can go wrong and why
If the oil turns rancid quickly, it is because the jars have been stored in direct sunlight, which also destroys the vitamins in the oil. The oil may also turn rancid if an already opened bottle of oil is used for preserving the foods. Always break the seal on a brand new bottle of oil so that you know it is fresh. If the contents of the jars start to become moldy, it could be because they are not completely covered with the oil.

GREEK OLIVES IN OIL

Olive oil, with its earthy aroma and flavor, is a perfect complement to the succulent Kalamata olive. It has a dual role in this recipe — to preserve the olives and absorb their flavor — so that once you have eaten the oil-soaked olives, you can use the scented oil for cooking.

INGREDIENTS

1 1/2 lb black Kalamata olives in brine

1 tsp coriander seeds

1 large sprig of fresh rosemary

1 1/4–1 1/2 cups extra-virgin olive oil

Makes about 1 quart

1 Drain the olives into a sieve and rinse them well under cold running water. Drain again and dry the olives thoroughly on paper towels.

2 ◄ Put the coriander seeds into a mortar and pestle and lightly crush them, being careful not to break them up completely. Alternatively, use the end of a rolling pin to break up the seeds.

3 ► Pack the olives into a sterilized jar, to within 3/4 inch of the top, adding the coriander as you go. Tuck the sprig of rosemary down one side of the jar.

4 ▲ Pour in the olive oil almost to the top of the jar, making sure all the olives are covered by 1/2 inch of oil. Use a metal skewer to push out air pockets.

5 Seal the jar and label. Keep in a cool dark place for at least 1 week before using to allow the flavors to develop.

RED-HOT LEMON SLICES IN OLIVE OIL

INGREDIENTS

6 lemons, total weight about
1 1/2 lb

3/4 cup sea salt

1–2 dried red chilies

2 bay leaves

2 Tb paprika

2/3 cup extra-virgin olive oil

1 Cut the lemons evenly into slices about 1/4 inch thick. Remove all the seeds from the slices.

2 Put the lemon slices in a single layer in a shallow nonmetallic dish. Sprinkle the slices with the salt, and leave to stand covered, for 24 hours to draw out the moisture.

3 Drain the lemon slices, leaving the salt on the surface. Roughly chop the chilies and crumble the bay leaves into small pieces. Mix them in a small bowl with the paprika.

4 Carefully pack the salt-encrusted lemon slices in neat layers into sterilized jars, to within 3/4 inch of the tops, sprinkling the spice mixture evenly between the layers as you go.

5 Pour in the oil almost to the tops of the jars, making sure that the lemons are covered by 1/2 inch of oil. Seal the jars and label. Keep in a cool dark place for at least 1 week before using to allow the flavors to develop.

Makes about 1 quart

SUN-DRIED TOMATOES IN OLIVE OIL

INGREDIENTS

1 cup whole sun-dried
tomatoes

2 bay leaves

3/4 cup olive oil

1 Put the sun-dried tomatoes in a bowl and pour boiling water over them just to cover. Leave for 5 minutes. Then drain in a plastic sieve and pat dry on paper towels.

2 Pack the tomatoes into sterilized jars to within 3/4 inch of the tops, tucking in the bay leaves as you go. Pour in the oil almost to the tops of the jars, making sure the tomatoes are covered by 1/2 inch of oil.

3 Seal the jars and label. Keep in a cool dark place for at least 2 weeks before using to allow the flavors to develop.

Makes about 1 1/2 cups

MUSHROOMS IN OIL

INGREDIENTS

1 1/2 lb button mushrooms

2 cups extra-virgin olive oil

juice of 4 lemons

12 peppercorns

3 garlic cloves

2 bay leaves

1 Remove and discard the stems from the mushrooms, and put the mushrooms in a bowl. Add half of the oil, and stir in the remaining ingredients. Leave to stand for 3–4 hours.

2 Pour the mushroom mixture into a saucepan and bring to a boil. Simmer, stirring occasionally, for 15 minutes. Remove from the heat and leave to cool.

3 Drain the mushrooms in a plastic sieve and pat dry on paper towels. Pack them into a sterilized jar, to within 3/4 inch of the top. Pour in the remaining oil almost to the top of the jar, making sure the mushrooms are covered by 1/2 inch.

4 Seal the jar, label, and refrigerate. Use within 2 weeks.

Makes about 1 quart

COOK'S TIP
Choose firm but moist mushrooms with no damp patches. Wipe them clean with damp paper towels before using.

Goat Cheese with Herbs in Oil

INGREDIENTS

2 small round goat cheeses, each weighing about 3 oz

3 sprigs of fresh thyme

3 bay leaves

6 peppercorns

scant 1 cup extra-virgin olive oil

Leaving the cheese for 2–3 weeks ensures that the oil takes on the full flavor of the cheese and vice versa. Use the cheese in salads or on crisp French bread, and the oil for cooking.

1 Cut each goat cheese into quarters. Pack the pieces into a sterilized jar, layering the cheese with the herbs and peppercorns as you go.

2 Pour in the olive oil to cover the cheese by $1/2$ inch.

3 Seal the jar and label. Keep in a cool dark place for 2–3 weeks before using to allow the flavors to develop.

Makes about 1$1/2$ cups

Provençal Olives in Aromatic Oil

INGREDIENTS

1$1/2$ lb green tanche olives, in brine

1 tsp fennel seeds

4 sprigs of fresh thyme

3 bay leaves

about 1$1/3$ cups extra-virgin olive oil

1 Drain the olives in a sieve and rinse them well under cold running water to remove any brine. Dry them on paper towels.

2 Pack the olives into a sterilized jar, sprinkling with the fennel seeds and tucking in the thyme and bay leaves as you go.

3 Slowly pour in the olive oil to cover the olives by $1/2$ inch. Use a metal skewer to push out any air pockets, taking care not to pierce the olives.

4 Seal the jar and label. Keep in a cool dark place for 1–2 weeks before using to allow the flavors to develop.

Makes about 1 quart

DID YOU KNOW?
Tanche olives are from Provence, in the south of France. If they are difficult to obtain, experiment with other green and black varieties.

Feta Cheese with Rosemary in Olive Oil

INGREDIENTS

6 oz feta cheese

4–6 sprigs of fresh rosemary

12 black peppercorns

12 black olives

scant 1 cup extra-virgin olive oil

1 Drain the cheese well and dry on paper towels. Cut the cheese into $3/4$ inch cubes.

2 Pack the cheese cubes into sterilized jars, to within $3/4$ inch of the tops, tucking in the rosemary, peppercorns, and olives as you go.

3 Pour in the olive oil to cover the cheese by $1/2$ inch.

4 Seal the jars and label. Keep in a cool dark place for at least 1 week before using to allow the flavors to develop.

Makes about 2 cups

GREEK TREAT
Serve Feta Cheese with Rosemary in Olive Oil as a light lunch dish with warm continental breads.

FLAVORED VINEGARS

COOKS AROUND the world have always welcomed vinegar into their kitchens, and have created endless roles for it to play. Through the art of pickling, it is a great preserver of nature's bounty, as well as a main ingredient for tenderizing tough meats, or making vinaigrette dressings for salads and crudités.

There are many basic types, from delicate Japanese rice vinegar through sharp wine vinegars to very robust malts, and exotic *aceto balsamico*. But add a variety of seasonings to flavor and color vinegars, and they take on a whole new guise. Herbs, fruits, and spices – all these can be steeped in vinegar. A dash of almost any sauce that has the blessing of a flavored vinegar will banish blandness and add piquancy to dishes such as soups, chowders, stews, and casseroles. Or use them combined with other seasonings to make marinades for meats, poultry, and seafood.

MAKING FLAVORED VINEGARS

❦ Sterilize the bottles (see page 11). Plain glass bottles are the best choice for flavored vinegars, to show off the color and flavorings of the vinegar inside. Dry the bottles thoroughly before using.

❦ Choose a good-quality vinegar with an acetic acid content of 5% or more. Malt vinegar can be used to make spiced vinegar for pickles, but choose wine, sherry, or cider vinegar to make flavored vinegars for using in salad dressings and for cooking.

❦ Select the flavorings. For herb vinegars, use fresh herbs, ideally picked before they flower. Use a single herb or several, mixing pungent and delicate ones together to balance the flavors. Fruit vinegars are usually made from soft fruits, such as raspberries, blueberries, or blackberries, or from citrus fruits. Other flavorings include garlic, dried chilies, and spices.

❦ Wash and dry the flavorings as necessary. The herbs, fruits, and spices may be crushed lightly to release more of their flavor.

❦ Insert the flavorings into the bottles, and add the vinegar almost to fill them.

❦ After sealing the bottles, the vinegar is left for about 2 weeks before using to allow the flavors to develop (unless the mixture is lightly cooked first, in which case the vinegar can be used immediately).

❦ Straining the vinegar after its initial storage ensures that it lasts longer and becomes more clear. You may need to strain the vinegar more than once to get a really clear liquid. After rebottling, a few fresh ingredients can be added for both decoration and identification. The bottles should then be resealed.

How to seal and store
Seal the bottles tightly with noncorrosive lids, plastic stoppers, or new corks. Corks are suitable only for short-term storage. After trimming corks to fit the bottles, sterilize them in boiling water for a few minutes; this also helps soften them slightly. To seal, gently pound the corks into the necks of the bottles with a mallet, leaving only 1/4 inch exposed cork.
Flavored vinegars should keep for about 12 months if the vinegar has been strained. However, if a large quantity of fresh herbs has been used and the vinegar has not been stained, the shelf life will be shorter (3–6 months). Vinegars that contain garlic may have a shorter shelf life.

What can go wrong and why
The vinegar can ferment if it is kept in too warm a place. Low storage temperature is important also for maintaining the flavor of the vinegar. Discard fermented vinegars or any that develop a questionable color or flavor. Vinegar can evaporate from the bottle if it has not been sealed tightly enough.

BLUEBERRY-HERB VINEGAR

Color and flavor pervade this distinguished vinegar, which combines plump blueberries, basil, and pink-tinted chive flowers. You can use one variety of basil, or a selection of sweet green and deep purple opal basil. For an elegant finishing touch, decant the vinegar into tall decorative bottles.

INGREDIENTS

1 large bunch of fresh basil

1 lb blueberries

4 cups white wine vinegar

1 Tb chopped fresh chives

fresh chive flowers and blueberries, for garnish

Makes about 3 2/3 cups

1 ▲ Strip the basil leaves from their stalks. Tear the leaves into small pieces.

2 ▲ Put the blueberries and a little vinegar into a nonmetallic bowl. Crush the berries with the back of a wooden spoon to release their juices.

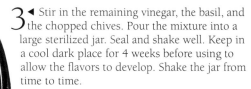

3 ◄ Stir in the remaining vinegar, the basil, and the chopped chives. Pour the mixture into a large sterilized jar. Seal and shake well. Keep in a cool dark place for 4 weeks before using to allow the flavors to develop. Shake the jar from time to time.

4 ► Line a funnel with a double layer of cheesecloth. Strain the flavored vinegar through it into sterilized bottles, to within 1/8 inch of the tops. Add a fresh chive flower and a few blueberries to each bottle to give an attractive garnish. Seal and label. The vinegar is now ready to use.

Herbs of Provence Vinegar

INGREDIENTS

*4 large sprigs of fresh
rosemary*

*4 large sprigs of fresh
tarragon*

4 sprigs of fresh thyme

6 fresh bay leaves

2 pinches of fennel seeds

4 cups red wine vinegar

Aromatic flavors from the south of France are combined here to give red wine vinegar a regional taste.

1 Lightly bruise the rosemary, tarragon, thyme, and bay leaves to release their flavors. Put all the herbs and the fennel seeds into a large sterilized jar, then pour in the vinegar.

2 Seal the jar and shake well. Keep in a cool dark place for 2–3 weeks before using to allow the flavors to develop. Shake the jar occasionally.

3 Line a funnel with a double layer of cheesecloth. Strain the flavored vinegar through it into sterilized bottles, to within 1/8 inch of the tops. Seal the bottles and label. The vinegar is now ready to use.

Makes about 1 quart

DID YOU KNOW?
The word vinegar comes from the French *vinaigre*, or sour wine. Half of the wine vinegar produced in France comes from the city of Orléans in the Loire valley.

Spiced Blackberry Vinegar

INGREDIENTS

2 lb blackberries

2 cinnamon sticks

2 tsp allspice berries

2 tsp whole cloves

2 1/3 cups vinegar

2 cups sugar

*a few fresh blackberries,
for garnish*

1 Pick over the blackberries, removing any moldy or damaged parts. Break the cinnamon sticks into pieces. Put all the spices on a square of cheesecloth and tie up with a piece of string.

2 Put the vinegar and sugar into a large saucepan. Stir over low heat, until the sugar has completely dissolved. Add the spice bag. Bring to a boil, lower the heat, and simmer for 5 minutes.

3 Add the blackberries and simmer for 10 minutes longer. Remove from the heat and leave the blackberry mixture to cool completely. Discard the spice bag.

4 Line a funnel with a double layer of cheesecloth. Strain the flavored vinegar through it into sterilized bottles, to within 1/8 inch of the tops. Add fresh blackberries to each bottle. Seal the bottles and label. The vinegar is now ready to use.

Makes about 1 quart

Orange-Scented Vinegar

INGREDIENTS

4 small oranges

4 cups white wine vinegar

*freshly peeled orange zest,
for garnish*

1 Thinly peel the zest from the oranges with a vegetable peeler, without taking off any pith. Cut the oranges in half and squeeze out the juice. Put the orange zest and juice into a sterilized jar, then pour in the vinegar.

2 Seal the jar and shake well. Keep in a cool dark place for at least 4 weeks before using to allow the flavors to develop. Shake the jar occasionally.

3 Line a funnel with a double layer of cheesecloth. Strain the flavored vinegar through it into sterilized bottles, to within 1/8 inch of the tops of the bottles.

4 Add 1–2 strips orange zest to each bottle. Seal the bottles and label. The vinegar is now ready to use.

Makes about 1 quart

GARLIC VINEGAR

INGREDIENTS

16 garlic cloves

salt

4 cups white or red wine vinegar

GARLIC STICK
For an unusual presentation thread 2–3 peeled garlic cloves on to a wooden skewer and drop into the bottle of garlic vinegar.

The flat side of a chef's knife can be used to crush garlic cloves. The granular texture of salt helps when crushing the cloves.

1 Peel the garlic cloves and crush with a little salt. Put the garlic into a large sterilized jar, then pour in the vinegar.

2 Seal the jar and shake well. Keep in a cool dark place for 2–3 weeks before using to allow the flavors to develop.

3 Line a funnel with a double layer of cheesecloth. Strain the flavored vinegar through it into the sterilized bottles, to within ¹/₈ inch of the tops of the bottles. Seal the bottles and label. The vinegar is now ready to use.

Makes about 1 quart

ROSEMARY AND ALLSPICE VINEGAR

INGREDIENTS

3–4 sprigs of fresh rosemary

1¹/₂ tsp allspice berries

2 cups red or white wine vinegar

1 Strip the rosemary leaves from their stalks. Lightly bruise the leaves to release their flavor. Put the allspice berries in a mortar and pestle and lightly crush them, being careful not to break them up completely. Alternatively, use the end of a rolling pin to crush them.

2 Put the rosemary and allspice into a sterilized jar, then pour in the vinegar. Seal the jar and shake well. Keep in a cool dark place for 4 weeks before using to allow the flavors to develop. Shake the jar occasionally.

3 Line a funnel with a double layer of cheesecloth. Strain the flavored vinegar through it into a sterilized bottle, to within ¹/₈ inch of the top. Seal the bottle and label. The vinegar is now ready to use.

Makes about 2 cups

SPICED PICKLING VINEGAR

INGREDIENTS

2 cinnamon sticks

2 blades of mace

4 tsp whole cloves

4 tsp allspice berries

1 Tb black peppercorns

4 cups cider vinegar

This vinegar is used to flavor vegetable pickles, chutneys, and even fruit pickles. It is also delicious when used with extra-virgin olive oil to make a vinaigrette dressing for salads.

1 Divide the cinnamon, mace, cloves, allspice, and peppercorns equally between 2 sterilized bottles. Pour in the vinegar, to within ¹/₈ inch of the tops of the bottles.

2 Seal the bottles and shake well. Label the bottles and keep in a cool dark place for 2 months before using to allow the flavors to develop. Shake the bottles occasionally.

Makes about 1 quart

COOK'S TIP You can use the vinegar in 24 hours rather than leaving it to mature, by heating it to just below boiling point, then pouring it over the spices. It has even more flavor if left for a week.

TARRAGON VINEGAR

INGREDIENTS

1 bunch of fresh tarragon

2 cups white wine vinegar

Fresh chervil can be substituted for tarragon in this recipe.

1 Lightly bruise the tarragon to release its flavor. Put the tarragon into a sterilized jar. Pour in the vinegar.

2 Seal the jar and shake well. Keep in a cool dark place for 2–3 weeks before using to allow the flavors to develop. Shake the jar occasionally.

3 Line a funnel with a double layer of cheesecloth. Strain the flavored vinegar through it into a sterilized bottle, to within 1/8 inch of the top. Seal the bottle and label. The vinegar is now ready to use.

Makes about 2 cups

BOUQUET OF HERBS VINEGAR

INGREDIENTS

4 large sprigs each of fresh parsley, rosemary, tarragon, and thyme

12 black peppercorns

4 celery sticks

4–6 shallots, depending on size

4 cups white wine vinegar

1 Lightly bruise the herbs to release their flavor. Lightly crush the peppercorns in a mortar and pestle, being careful not to break them up completely. Alternatively, use the end of a rolling pin to crush them. Thinly slice the celery and shallots.

2 Put all the flavorings into a large sterilized jar, then pour in the vinegar. Seal the jar and shake well. Keep in a cool dark place for 2–3 weeks before using to allow the flavors to develop. Shake the jar occasionally.

3 Line a funnel with a double layer of cheesecloth. Strain the flavored vinegar through it into sterilized bottles, to within 1/8 inch of the tops. Seal and label the bottles. The vinegar is now ready to use.

Makes about 1 quart

ROSY RASPBERRY VINEGAR

INGREDIENTS

1 lb raspberries

2 cups white wine vinegar

1/4 cup sugar

a few fresh raspberries, for garnish

This is a concentrated vinegar that should be used sparingly. The addition of raspberries yields a delicious flavor and color.

1 Pick over the raspberries and remove any moldy or bruised parts. Put the berries and a little vinegar into a nonmetallic bowl. Crush the berries with the back of a wooden spoon to release their juices. Stir in the remaining vinegar.

2 Pour the mixture into a sterilized jar. Seal the jar and shake well. Keep in a cool dark place for 2–3 weeks before using to allow the flavors to develop. Shake the jar occasionally.

3 Line a funnel with a double layer of cheesecloth. Strain the flavored vinegar through it into a small saucepan. Stir in the sugar and simmer over low heat for 10 minutes. Allow to cool.

4 Pour the sweetened vinegar into a sterilized bottle, to within 1/8 inch of the top. Add a few fresh raspberries to the bottle. Seal the bottle and label. The vinegar is now ready to use.

Makes about 1 1/4 cups

HERBS & SPICES

HERB & SPICE BLENDS

HERBS AND SPICES add flavor and variety to foods, that would be very dull without them. Herbs have many virtues: they contribute vitamins to our daily fare, they originate from all over the world but seldom fail to adapt to different soils and climates, and they often have a natural culinary affinity for each other. The classic combination of herbs found in most kitchens – a few sprigs of parsley, a sprig of thyme, and a bay leaf, all tied together with a piece of thread or string – is known by French chefs as a *bouquet garni*. If the herbs are dried they are wrapped in a square of cheesecloth and tied with string. Another popular combination in France is *herbes de Provence*, a mixture of the herbs that grow in the hills of this southern region of France. The mixture is especially good in dishes from the Mediterranean.

Spices, close kitchen companions of herbs, are more robustly flavored and more exotic because many are from the tropics. Although very different in nature, they combine successfully with sugar. Spices are also essential to pickling; they are used in cakes and cookies, to flavor wine punches, and particularly in Asian cooking. They are an essential component of curries and season cuisines worldwide. Herb and spice blends give every cook a veritable battalion of kitchen condiments for livening up their dishes.

MAKING HERB & SPICE BLENDS

❦ Select the ingredients. Buy herbs and spices at a store where you know there is a high turnover, so that they are always fresh. If possible, grow and dry your own herbs.
❦ Prepare the herbs or spices. Crumble dried herbs between your fingers or crush them with a rolling pin. Large amounts are easier to crush if put in a plastic bag first. Process dried spices in a mortar and pestle or in an electric grinder. Alternatively, the end of a rolling pin can be used to crush spices. This treatment also helps to prevent peppercorns, allspice berries, and coriander seeds from getting stuck in the blades of the grinder. Occasionally, the herbs and spices are toasted in a dry skillet before they are ground; this helps to extract the full flavor of the ingredients.
❦ Mix the herbs or spices in a bowl. Do not stir too vigorously, or the powders will make you sneeze. Spoon the mixture into small sterilized jars (see page 11), packing it down well by tapping the bottom of the jar on the work surface. A handmade funnel placed in the top of the jar makes the job of spooning in spices easier.

How to seal and store
Seal the jars tightly with screw-top lids. These are the best choice for keeping herb and spice blends fresh. Corks trimmed to fit the necks of the jars can also be used, and they look attractive, but the spices will lose their flavor more quickly. Keep the jars in a cool dark place, for up to 4–6 months for herb and spice blends, and up to 1 year for flavored sugars.

What can go wrong and why
If the herb and spice blends lose their color and flavor, they have been stored for too long or incorrectly.
Unless they are kept in dry conditions in truly airtight containers, the flavored salts and sugars will become compact and will not pour freely.

Aromatic Garam Masala

The blending of spices is an integral part of all Indian cooking. In Northern India, the most important mixture of spices is known as garam masala: "masala" literally mean a "blend." Each cook creates his or her own blend, making it fiercely fiery or subtly aromatic, from a selection of two or three spices to sometimes over a dozen. This mild mix, dominated by the scent of cardamom, is ideal for meat curries.

Ingredients

20 green cardamom pods

3 cinnamon sticks

4 dried bay leaves

2 Tb black peppercorns

4 tsp cumin seeds

2 tsp whole cloves

2 tsp freshly grated nutmeg

Makes about 1/3 cup

1 Split open the cardamom pods with a small sharp knife and remove the dark brown seeds. Discard the pods and crush the seeds in a mortar and pestle. Alternatively, use the end of a rolling pin to crush them.

2 ◄With your fingers, break the cinnamon sticks into fairly small lengths. Crumble each dried bay leaf into several small pieces.

Stir and shake the pan frequently when frying the spices, to keep them on the move and prevent them from burning

3 ▶ Put all the spices, except the nutmeg, into a skillet. Dry-fry them over a medium heat for 2–3 minutes. Remove the pan from the heat and put the spices into a small bowl. Allow to cool, and stir in the grated nutmeg.

4 ◄Put the spices, in small batches, into an electric grinder and grind to a fine powder. (Traditionally, masalas are ground in a mortar and pestle, but an electric grinder is quicker and easier.) Pack the spice mix into a sterilized jar, seal, and label.

KASHMIRI MASALA

INGREDIENTS

8 green cardamom pods

1 cinnamon stick

2 Tb cumin seeds

1 Tb black peppercorns

2 tsp whole cloves

2 tsp caraway seeds

1 tsp freshly grated nutmeg

The fragrance of cardamom permeates Kashmiri Masala, a blend of spices from the northernmost valleys of India. Green cardamoms have the most delicate flavor, while the brown have an unpleasant taste and should not be used. This masala is good for chicken and lamb curries.

1 Remove the seeds from the cardamom pods and crush them in a mortar and pestle. Alternatively, use the end of a rolling pin. Break the cinnamon stick into several pieces.

2 Put all the spices, except the nutmeg, into a skillet and dry-fry over medium heat for 2–3 minutes. Allow to cool.

3 Put the whole spices, and the nutmeg, into an electric grinder and grind to a fine powder. Alternatively, use a mortar and pestle. Pack into a sterilized jar, seal, and label.

Makes about 1/2 cup

CHAAT MASALA

INGREDIENTS

6 dried red chilies

6 Tb cumin seeds

6 Tb coriander seeds

4 tsp black peppercorns

"Dry-frying" whole spices in a skillet to a dark brown color before grinding, as in this masala recipe, extracts their full flavor and heightens their aroma.

1 Break the chilies into pieces. Dry-fry all the spices in a skillet over medium heat until the seeds start to pop and color. This takes 2–3 minutes. Remove them from the heat so that they do not burn. Allow to cool.

2 Put all the spices into an electric grinder, and grind to a fine powder. Alternatively, use a mortar and pestle. Pack into a sterilized jar, seal and label.

Makes about 1/3 cup

PICKLING SPICE

INGREDIENTS

4 blades of mace

2 cinnamon sticks

2 small dried red chilies

2 small pieces of dried gingerroot

2 Tb allspice berries

2 Tb whole cloves

2 Tb coriander seeds

2 Tb mustard seeds

2 Tb black or white peppercorns

In European cooking, the idea of mixing different spices together to make a blend has fallen from favor over the years, with cooks preferring to use spices individually. One of the mixes that has retained its popularity is Pickling Spice, used to liven up the flavor of chutneys, pickles, relishes, and spiced vinegars.

1 Break the mace blades, cinnamon sticks, and chilies into pieces, and chop the gingerroot. Put all the spices into a bowl and stir. Pack into a sterilized jar, seal, and label.

2 To use, put a spoonful of spices on a square of cheesecloth and tie up tightly with a long piece of string. Add to the recipe when specified. Remove the bag after pickling.

Makes about 2 3/4 cups

VARIATION Proportions and types of spices for this traditional English recipe can vary. Fennel seeds can be added, and a pinch of freshly grated nutmeg can replace the mace.

Five-Spice Powder

INGREDIENTS

2 cinnamon sticks

6 star anise

2 Tb whole cloves

1 Tb fennel seeds

1 Tb anise seeds

When blended together according to an ancient formula, these five spices create a harmonious mix of bitter, sweet, sour, and salty flavors. The pungent taste of five-spice powder permeates many Chinese and Vietnamese roast meat and poultry dishes.

1 Break the cinnamon sticks into several pieces.

2 Put all the spices into an electric grinder and grind to a fine powder. Alternatively, use a mortar and pestle.

3 Pack into a sterilized jar, seal, and label.

Makes about 1/4 cup

VARIATION Szechuan pepper or black peppercorns can be used instead of the anise seeds.

Quatre Epices

INGREDIENTS

3 Tb white peppercorns

1 tsp whole cloves

4 tsp freshly grated nutmeg

1 Tb ground ginger

Like the Pickling Spice mix, this French blend of four spices can vary in its composition. Allspice and cinnamon make good substitutes for the other spices in this recipe.

1 Put the peppercorns and cloves into an electric grinder and grind to a fine powder. Alternatively, use a mortar and pestle.

2 Put the mixture into a bowl and mix with the nutmeg and the ground ginger.

3 Pack into a sterilized jar, seal, and label.

Makes about 5 Tb

Dill Pickle Spices

INGREDIENTS

2 small red chilies

4 dried bay leaves

1 small piece of dried gingerroot

3 Tb mustard seeds

1 Tb dill seeds

1 Tb coriander seeds

2 tsp black peppercorns

1 tsp allspice berries

1 tsp whole cloves

1/2 tsp fennel seeds

The dainty dill seed, with a flavor reminiscent of caraway, is the special ingredient for Dill Pickle Spices. Use this blend for pickled cucumber or dill pickles, pickled sour gherkins, or in flavored vinegars.

1 Break the chilies and bay leaves into pieces. Chop the gingerroot. Mix all the spices in a bowl.

2 Pack into a sterilized jar, seal, and label.

Makes about 1/2 cup

Left to right,
Quatre Epices,
Kashmiri
Masala, Dill
Pickle Spices

ALL-AMERICAN BARBECUE BLEND

INGREDIENTS

2 Tb each of dried parsley and chives

1 Tb each of dried mint, thyme, and tarragon

2 Tb freshly ground black pepper

1 tsp paprika

1 Put all the ingredients into a bowl and mix together well, making sure to lightly crush the dried herbs into several pieces.

2 Pack into a sterilized jar. Seal the jar and label. The barbecue blend is now ready to use.

Makes about 1/3 cup

VARIATIONS Different dried herbs and spices, such as rosemary, cumin, and chili, can be used to make this mix. Other flavorings like honey and mustard can also be added to the mix, which is sprinkled directly on to meat and poultry while barbecuing.

SEVEN SEAS SPICE BLEND

INGREDIENTS

15 green cardamom pods

1 cinnamon stick

2 Tb coriander seeds

2 small dried red chilies

1 Tb cumin seeds

2 tsp each of celery seeds and whole cloves

This fragrant blend is an excellent flavoring for Indonesian, Malaysian, and Korean dishes.

1 Remove the seeds from the cardamom pods and crush them in a mortar and pestle. Alternatively, use the end of a rolling pin. Break the cinnamon stick into several pieces.

2 Put all of the spices into an electric grinder and grind to a fine powder. Alternatively, use a mortar and pestle. Pack the spice mixture into a sterilized jar. Seal the jar and label. The spice blend is now ready to use.

Makes about 1/2 cup

TARRAGON SALT

INGREDIENTS

1 bunch of fresh tarragon

1/2 cup sea salt

1 Set the oven to its lowest temperature. Strip the tarragon leaves from the stalks. Discard the stalks. Coarsely chop the leaves and mix with the salt in a blender until the leaves are finely chopped.

2 Spread the leaves out on a baking tray covered with aluminum foil. Put in the oven with the door ajar and leave for 1 1/2 hours, or until crisp and dry. Allow to cool.

3 Pack the salt into sterilized jars. Seal the jars and label. The tarragon salt is now ready to use.

Makes about 1/2 cup

SEASONING SALT

INGREDIENTS

6 Tb sea salt

1 1/2 tsp each of ground celery seeds, white pepper, cumin, and paprika or cayenne pepper

This is an important condiment for marinating meats.

1 Put all the ingredients into a bowl and mix together well.

2 Pack into sterilized jars. Seal the jars and label. The seasoning salt is now ready to use.

Makes about 1/2 cup

ITALIAN SEASONING

INGREDIENTS

8–12 dried bay leaves

3 Tb each of dried oregano, parsley, thyme, and sage

3 Tb each of freshly ground black pepper and paprika

1 Crush the dried bay leaves with a rolling pin until they are broken into quite fine pieces. Alternatively, use a mortar and pestle. Put them with all the remaining ingredients into a bowl and mix together well.

2 Pack into a sterilized jar. Seal the jar and label. The Italian seasoning is now ready to use.

Makes about 1 cup

HERBES DE PROVENCE

INGREDIENTS

¹/4 cup each of dried oregano, savory, thyme, marjoram, and rosemary

In Provence, dried herbes de Provence are sold in little terra-cotta pots topped with the local patterned cloth, or in brightly colored bags of the same material. By simply blending five herbs, you can make your own mixture, for adding authenticity to Provençal dishes.

1 Put all of the herbs into a bowl and mix together well.

2 Pack into a sterilized jar. Seal the jar and label. The herbs are now ready to use.

Makes about 1¹/4 cups

BOUQUET GARNI

INGREDIENTS

12 dried bay leaves

¹/4 cup dried thyme

¹/4 cup dried parsley

2 Tb dried celery leaves

This French blend is usually tied together in a cheesecloth square when dried ingredients are used. The bundle should always contain a bay leaf, thyme, and parsley. Sometimes other herbs, like chervil, savory, or tarragon, are added. Celery leaves can also be used.

1 Crush the bay leaves with a rolling pin until they are broken into quite fine pieces. Alternatively, use a mortar and pestle. Put them with the remaining herbs into a bowl and mix together.

2 Cut a double layer of cheesecloth into 3 inch squares. Put 1 Tb herb mixture on each square and tie up tightly into a bag with string. Pack the bags into sterilized jars. Seal the jars and label. The bouquets garnis are now ready to use.

Makes enough for 12 cheesecloth bags

ENGLISH MIXED HERBS

INGREDIENTS

6 Tb each of dried parsley, chives, thyme, and tarragon

This is the English version of herbes de Provence. It is a wonderful complement for lamb, pork, or stuffing. Rosemary, sage, and marjoram can also be used in addition or as substitutes.

1 Put all of the herbs into a bowl and mix together well.

2 Pack into a sterilized jar. Seal the jar and label. The mixed herbs are now ready to use.

Makes about 1¹/2 cups

SPICE BLEND

INGREDIENTS

2 cinnamon sticks

2 Tb coriander seeds

2 tsp allspice berries

2 tsp whole cloves

1¹/₂ Tb ground ginger

1 tsp freshly grated nutmeg

This blend is also known as pie spice, and has been popular since the 16th century. Few traditional mixtures have survived as long. Use it in pies, cakes, and cookies.

1 Break the cinnamon sticks into several pieces. Put along with the coriander, allspice, and cloves into an electric grinder and grind to a fine powder. Alternatively, use a mortar and pestle.

2 Put the spice mixture into a bowl and stir in the ginger and nutmeg. Pack into a sterilized jar. Seal the jar and label. The spices are now ready to use.

Makes about ¹/₃ cup

VANILLA SUGAR

INGREDIENTS

4 cups sugar

4 vanilla beans

As this vanilla sugar is used up, in custards, cakes, and dessert sauces, keep the jar filled with fresh sugar. It will continue to absorb the vanilla flavor from the beans.

1 Divide the sugar between 2 sterilized jars. Press 2 vanilla beans down into the sugar in each jar.

2 Seal the jars and label. Keep in a cool dark place for 1 week before using to allow the flavors to develop.

Makes about 4 cups

CINNAMON SUGAR

INGREDIENTS

4 cups sugar

about 5 cinnamon sticks

1 Divide the sugar between 2 sterilized jars. Divide the whole cinnamon sticks evenly between the jars and press the sticks down into the sugar.

2 Seal the jars and label. Keep in a cool dark place for 1 week before using to allow the flavors to develop.

Makes about 4 cups

ORANGE OR LEMON SUGAR

INGREDIENTS

6 oranges or 8 lemons

2 lb sugar

1 Set the oven to its lowest temperature. Peel the zest from the fruit with a vegetable peeler. Spread the zest out on a baking tray covered with aluminum foil. Put in the oven and leave for 3 hours or until dried out. Let the zest cool.

2 Divide the sugar between 2 sterilized jars, layering it with the dried zest. Seal the jars and label. Keep in a cool dark place for 1 week before using to allow the flavors to develop.

Makes about 4 cups

Spice Blend for Mulled Cider

INGREDIENTS

6 cinnamon sticks

*12 pieces of dried lemon zest
(see box, page 110)*

6 whole nutmegs, cut in half

36 whole cloves

To make mulled cider: use 1 bag of spice mix for each 2¹/₂ cups cider.

1 Cut a double layer of cheesecloth into 12 pieces, each 2 inches by 3 inches.

2 Break each cinnamon stick into 2 pieces. Put 1 piece each of cinnamon stick and lemon zest with half a nutmeg and 3 cloves, on each piece of cheesecloth. Gather the cheesecloth into small bundles and tie up tightly into bags with string. Pack the bags into sterilized jars. Seal the jars and label. The spice bags are now ready to use.

Makes enough for 12 cheesecloth bags

Spice Blend for Glühwein

INGREDIENTS

*24 small pieces of dried
gingerroot*

6 Tb allspice berries

24 whole cloves

This German spice blend is traditionally used to make Glühwein.

1 Put all of the spices into a bowl, and mix together well.

2 Pack into sterilized jars. Seal the jars and label. The spice blend is now ready to use.

Makes ¹/₂ cup

To Make Glühwein Pour 2 bottles of red wine into a saucepan, and add 3 Tb sugar. Simmer over low heat, stirring with a wooden spoon, until the sugar has completely dissolved. Do not allow the mixture to boil. Add 3 Tb *Glühwein* spices, 1 sliced orange, and 1 sliced lemon. Heat to just below boiling. Taste and add more sugar, if necessary. Leave the *Glühwein* to stand for 1 hour, then reheat and serve. Makes 6–8 servings.

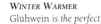

WINTER WARMER
Glühwein *is the perfect
beverage when the
weather is cold.*

Orange Spice Blend

INGREDIENTS

12 cinnamon sticks

24 whole cloves

3 Tb allspice berries

*12 pieces of dried orange
zest (see box, page 110)*

Infuse this blend in hot or cold wine, cider, tea, or lemonade punches.

1 Break each cinnamon stick into 2 pieces. Put with the remaining ingredients into a bowl and mix together well.

2 Pack into sterilized jars. Seal the jars and label. The spice blend is now ready to use.

Makes about 1¹/₂ cups

Cook's Tip When infusing these spices in punches, allow 2 Tb mixture for each 2¹/₂ cups liquid. Tie up the spices into a cheesecloth bag so they will flavor the punch without having to be strained out.

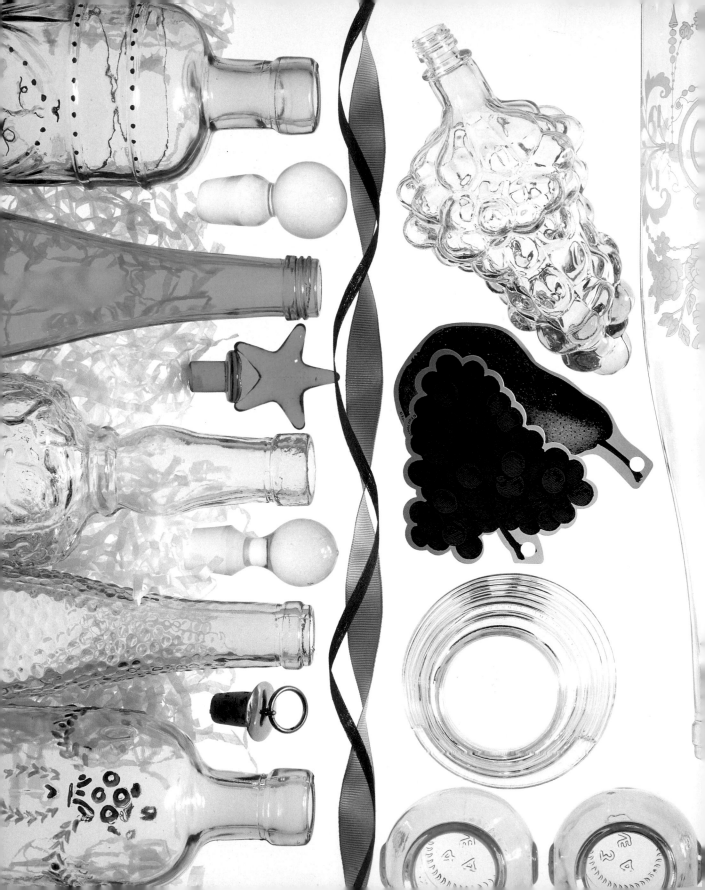

FINISHING
TOUCHES

DECORATING BOTTLES

Glass bottles can be transformed into rustic, romantic, vibrant, or psychedelic creations by a little paintwork, stenciling, or spraying. All you need are metallic spray paints, waterproof felt-tip pens, sable-hair brushes, and specially formulated glass paints, which are all available at good craft shops. Use clean dry bottles so that the paint will adhere properly. Handmade paper collars are an eye-catching finishing touch.

Above left, *handpainted bottle;* **above right**, *negative stenciled bottle*

POSITIVE STENCILING
Affix a stencil to the bottle and spray with metallic spray paint, to simulate an etched or antique glass effect. Be sure to cover and protect all other surfaces of the bottle with adhesive tape, surrounding surfaces with newspaper and your hands with rubber gloves. When the paint is dry, remove the tape and stencil. Any blurred edges can be cleaned up with a razor blade or with a little nail polish remover.

NEGATIVE STENCILING
Apply self-adhesive stickers, or shapes made from masking tape, all around the bottle to create a pattern. Stick the edges down well, or paint will seep underneath. Protect the top of the bottle with tape. Spray the entire bottle with metallic spray paint, leave for 30 minutes, and spray with a second coat. When the paint is dry, carefully remove the stickers to reveal the pattern on the bottle.

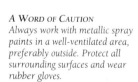

A WORD OF CAUTION
Always work with metallic spray paints in a well-ventilated area, preferably outside. Protect all surrounding surfaces and wear rubber gloves.

PAINTING BOTTLES

Use formulated glass paints or waterproof felt-tip pens to decorate bottles. Try simple patterns before graduating to more complicated designs. Apply the paints in one stroke because they dry quickly. Some thinners that delay drying times are available, but use sparingly. Highlight the design on the bottle by attaching white paper or cardboard to the other side, then remove the paper for the finishing touches. Delicate handpainted surfaces can be protected with a coat of clear craft varnish.

FINISHING TOUCHES
Silk ribbons and braids look beautiful tied around bottles; they are also useful for attaching tags and covers to the bottles.

MAKING COVERS AND COLLARS

Covers for bottles can be made with material or metallic crêpe paper. Cut a circle from the material or paper and tie it on the bottle with a large ribbon or cord. Collars, made from cardboard, are more difficult: draw a template in the shape shown below, on the back of some colored cardboard. Cut out the template. Lightly score along the dotted lines and bend the cardboard. Glue or tape the angled end to the inside of the opposite end to fasten, and slip over the bottle neck.

PRETTY AS A PICTURE
Spray-painted and handpainted bottles look artistic when finished with a collar or decorated with leaves and braiding.

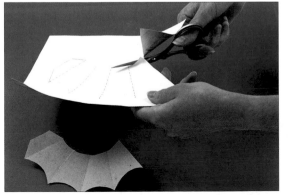

DECORATING JARS

Great gift wrapping does not need to cost a fortune. Liven up a humble jar with a spray of découpage cherries, a leaf-wrapped lid, or a bright strip of grosgrain ribbon sealed with wax. Alternatively, a cotton bandeau ribbon or a silk cord can be tied around the jar to make it look extra special.

DÉCOUPAGE
Decorating surfaces with paper cutouts is known as découpage. Cut out fruit or vegetable pictures from magazines, keeping the edges neat (a thin artist's knife is best for this task). Coat the back of the cut out with paper adhesive, and position decoratively on the jar or lid.

PICTURESQUE PRESERVES
Paper cutouts can turn preserves into fancy gifts. They look beautiful and also indicate what is inside.

COVERING LIDS WITH LEAVES
Wash and dry large leaves, such as Virginia creeper, sycamore, or maple. Paint the leaves on both sides with glycerine (available from drugstores). Arrange them on the top of a lid, wrap in plastic wrap, and secure with a rubber band. Weight the lid and leave in the refrigerator overnight. Gently unwrap and wipe off any excess glycerine. Secure the leaf on the lid with a piece of raffia.

MAKING A WAX SEAL

Wrap ribbon around the jar and hold temporarily in place with masking tape. Use a taper to light a stick of sealing wax and hold it about 1 inch away from the point to be sealed. Let wax drip steadily until a 1 inch wide blob has formed. If the flame goes out, relight the wax and continue. Before the wax has time to cool, press a decorative metal seal down firmly on the melted wax, and hold it there for a few seconds until a good impression has been left. Remove the masking tape.

Note: it is a good idea to practice making your seals beforehand with some spare ribbon on empty jars.

SEALING WITH WAX

A variety of decorative metal seals and wax sticks are available from specialist stationery shops.

__Far right__, wax seals add a professional touch to gifts; __right__, leaf-wrapped lids are a natural-looking covering for jars.

PRESENTATION IDEAS

*Beautifully presented preserves are a pleasure both to give
and to receive. Here are some imaginative and innovative ways
to make your gifts look elegant and stylish.*

ALL WRAPPED UP
Make your own gift bags with wallpaper
and string and place preserves inside in a
straw "nest." Alternatively, cover with
unbleached linen and tie with raffia.

IN THE BAG
Use clear paper glue to stick
shells and starfish onto
bottle bags. Rest bottles in
shredded tissue.

HAT TRICK
Wrap hair netting around
the bottle and secure with
florist's wire. Decorate with
braid and ribbon.

A TOUCH OF SPICE
Spice bags are made of
cheesecloth tied with
ribbons and strings
for gift giving.
Place several bags in
a glass and wrap with
patterned cellophane.
Bundle up with a bow.

A BEAUTIFUL BOX
Cover boxes with designer
paper, pleating the edges.
Use doilies and tissue to
create a lavish effect.

PERFECT FIT
Cover a storage tin and lid with wood-patterned paper, snipping and folding pleats over the edges, so they are neat. Adorn with silken braid and gingham tissue paper.

BANDANA WRAP
Bandanas are useful and ornamental. Knot around preserves in a basket.

POPPING SUCCESS
Cellophane "poppers" are a good way to display jars of preserves, herbs, and spices.

BREAKFAST BUNDLE
Set a jar of jam on shredded tissue inside a cup and saucer, then wrap in cellophane and tie with ribbon.

BASKET WORK
Wood or straw baskets look attractively rustic. Lay preserves on a bed of straw and secure in place with wire.

LABELS & TAGS

Decorate your gifts with a label or a tag to provide a personal touch to your culinary creations. Commercial labels, tags, and lids are available, but it is easy to design and make your own. A calligraphy pen can be used to write on tags.

DESIGN A TAG
Draw or paint a tag to reflect the ingredients in your preserves, to give instant recognition of their flavorings.

HANDPAINTED LABELS
Use nature as an inspiration to create beautiful handpainted labels. Affix to your bottles or jars with glue or double-sided tape.

TEMPLATE TAGS
Use a template, such as a leaf or a traced illustration, to make pretty shapes. Use colored or embossed paper and cut edges with pinking shears for added interest.

EMBOSSED TAGS
Use specialized embossing tools, such as a template and a stylus, to press out the initials of the recipient of your gift.

COMMERCIAL GOODS
Labels, tags, and jar covers are available in stores, so search around for the latest designs.

HAND TINTED TAGS
Take photocopies of fruit or vegetable illustrations and hand-tint with crayons, colored pens, or pencils.

ACKNOWLEDGMENTS

Photographers David Murray
Jules Selmes
Photographer's Assistant Steven Head
Home Economist Sarah Lowman
Typesetting Debbie Lelliott
Linda Parker
Debbie Rhodes
US Editors Jeanette Mall
Chris Benton
Julee Binder

Production Consultant Lorraine Baird
Text film by Disc to Print (UK) Limited

Carroll & Brown Ltd would like to thank Stephen Poole, Mary
Denning, Pat Baines, and Audrey Fox for supplying produce from
their gardens for photography, and Carolyn Chapman for her help
with the Finishing Touches chapter. A selection of decorative ribbons
was supplied by Panda Ribbons. Labels on pages 132 and 137 are
copyright of Kate Weese, California.

NOTES

•Preserving is not without dangers. Cleanliness,
equipment, timing, acidity, and a wide variety of other
factors are critical to getting results that are safe to eat.
The foods shown in this book were decanted and
photographed immediately after preparation; they are not
all in airtight containers. This book gives recipes and
guidelines only. If you wish to store foods for longer
periods, you must follow specific instructions for methods
of preserving. For additional information, contact your
Department of Agriculture Cooperative Extension Service.
Dorling Kindersley assumes no responsibility for the
preserving of foods described in this book.

•Over a period of prolonged storage, the colors of some of
the preserves may fade.